Registered for Life

Registered for Life

Consequences of a former sex offender

R LUTHER COOPER

authorHOUSE®

AuthorHouse™
1663 Liberty Drive
Bloomington, IN 47403
www.authorhouse.com
Phone: 1-800-839-8640

This book is a work of non-fiction. Unless otherwise noted, the author and the publisher make no explicit guarantees as to the accuracy of the information contained in this book and in some cases, names of people and places have been altered to protect their privacy.

First published by AuthorHouse   01/09/2012

ISBN: 978-1-4685-0039-4 (sc)
ISBN: 978-1-4685-0038-7 (hc)
ISBN: 978-1-4685-0037-0 (ebk)

Library of Congress Control Number: 2011960283

Printed in the United States of America

Any people depicted in stock imagery provided by Thinkstock are models, and such images are being used for illustrative purposes only.
Certain stock imagery © Thinkstock.

This book is printed on acid-free paper.

Because of the dynamic nature of the Internet, any web addresses or links contained in this book may have changed since publication and may no longer be valid. The views expressed in this work are solely those of the author and do not necessarily reflect the views of the publisher, and the publisher hereby disclaims any responsibility for them.

Dedication

To my loving, wonderful wife who heals my shame, supports my efforts and harbors me from this cruel outside world. Thank you for your unconditional love and for giving me the courage to fight back from the brink of ruin many times.

To my grown children and their families, forgive me for all of the hurt you endure at my expense. The embarrassment and shame you did not deserve from the fate of growing up a child of a registered sex offender father. You got a raw deal and deserve better. In spite of all that has happened, thank you for your continued love.

Acknowledgments

I want to thank Alyssa for editing my mess.

I want to thank my "staff" of Rachel, my neighbor Hazel, one of my favorite cooks, Julie, who keeps me in sandwiches and specials down at the local hang-out. Also, thank you to Ramona for not throwing me out of the place and the rest of the rowdies who are supposed to be working for her.

Thanks to my newest sister-in-law Susan bored enough in New Mexico to review my scribbles and who shot back some insightful comments.

Thanks to the "review crew", my brother Gary and Blanca for enduring my earliest manuscripts and bouncing back some changes.

I'm indebted to all of you for your time and encouragement.

A very SPECIAL thank you goes to Sharon for helping in every aspect of this effort and dealing with my challenge of the English language. You are loved.

Lastly, least I forget (which I proudly do now that I've attained a certain age), my greatest gratitude goes to the ONE I met some 42 years ago who knocked on my heart's door and I let HIM in. I look forward to seeing in the here-after, whose love and power sustains me daily.

1

My journey began back in the summer of 1951 when I became the first child of both of my parents' second marriages. During my first five pre-school years we lived in a small farming town with a population of about 3,000 in the middle of the Central Valley in California. My mother and older step-brother (by five years) had come to the Valley from the San Francisco Bay area (following her divorce) to live with her older brother (my uncle) Steve[1] and his wife (my aunt) Susan. Uncle Steve was fifteen years older than my mom and had established himself as a heavy equipment mechanic. He and his wife had two daughters (my cousins) Grace and Virginia. They had moved to this small town and built their own home just a few blocks away from the home in which my father was born and raised. Uncle Steve, being more than just a mechanic, had built a smaller second home on the back of his property. His retired parents (my grandma and grandpa) lived in it.

---

[1] This is a true story however all the names have been changed to protect the identities of the people mentioned

I remember grandma's house as a quaint little cottage behind my uncle's "big castle" guarded by a big black dog that, of course, scared the heck outta little boys. But I cherish those wonderful childhood memories of the many times I was allowed (as a five year old kindergarten kid and "big enough") to venture *all on my own* through the "big forest" of sycamore trees (between the sidewalk and curbs) full of big, bad, *imaginary wolves* and hop-scotch skip along the sidewalk to Grandma's house, a couple of blocks away. I'd feast on freshly baked bread with **real** butter and home-made jam or those special warm cookies that only Grandmas know the secret to making. My grandma was a small framed, short, rather stocky woman, warm and loving with an infectious smile. She made me feel special. It seemed she had all day to spend time with me while my mother was busy with two of my younger brothers, one still in diapers.

When my parents first met, my mom was a young single mother working as a waitress at the local bakery/coffee shop just a few blocks' walk from her home. My dad was a veteran of three tours of duty with the Marines in the Pacific during World War II. He was a decorated veteran and surviving **three** tours then was unheard of. In fact, prior to his last deployment he gave away all his worldly belongings declaring that "nobody comes home a third time."

Sounds like we're heading in the direction of some "forties war hero meets the young, struggling waitress (damsel in distress) and rides in on his white horse (1939 coupe) to rescue her (and the kid), fall madly in love and live happily ever after" crappy movie. There probably were some elements of that. But the reality was she was alone, trying to raise her child and had many fears about her unsettled future hoping for the "dream" and in need of serious emotional healing. He was a returning soldier (I mean Marine—they hate being called soldiers) trying to start a career while stuffing his war experiences and, in my opinion, suffering from what is now called Post Traumatic Stress Disorder (PTSD)[2]. In those days, a *real man* certainly didn't talk about that sort of thing. During the summer that I turned six we moved to a larger small town with a population of 13,000 about 25 miles away. My dad was a railroad engineer and we were able to afford a *brand new, sub-division* home close to his work and within walking distance to public schools. We were part of the emerging middle-class, post-war, "baby boom" suburban

---

[2] PTSD, www.ptsdmanual.com/chap1.htm

expansion taking place all over the country. I showed up on the first day at my new school with the usual Dad-inflicted *buzz* haircut, a button-downed farmer-plaid shirt, Penny's "plain pocket" jeans and a pair of Redwing boots all ready to "get an education." Our family prospered and grew with the addition of another brother and (at last) my little sister, the princess. So you see. I was raised in a middle-class family from a typical small town with my older and three younger brothers and a younger sister. We had plenty of the things it took to live in middle-class America in the 50's and 60's. We all went to public schools back when they had structure and discipline. I was taught most importantly that I was fortunate to live right smack in the middle of the Great Central Valley of California in the heart of America, the greatest country in the world!

Only as I grew older did I realize how special a place it was to grow up in. On any summer day we could just go down the road and get our own fresh strawberries, cherries, peaches, tomatoes, corn or watermelon, you name it, directly from the farmers. We could jump in the car and in minutes be out boating in the Delta waterways or go down to the local public swimming pool. Adding to all that, we were only a few hours drive to the Sierras for some of the greatest mountain camping in the entire world. I could ride my bike all over town, day or night, without any fear. Doors were left unlocked. To me it was a lot like "Mayberry." I had the privileges of playing Little League baseball, to be in Cub and Boy Scouts (I'm an Eagle Scout), to play sports in high school (earning four varsity letters) and all-in-all had a **NORMAL** up-bringing.

So for those of you who picked up this book with the notion that a Registered *Sex Offender* can't possibly be NORMAL and certainly must be the result of a horrible childhood or the victim of some heinous act or even, God forbid, was just born that way, I'm sorry to disappoint you. That would be too easy. One of the biggest reasons that I'm writing this book is to show how subtle and destructive the "sins of the father" can be visited upon the sons for generations to come, especially in normal families.

My offensive behavior was not a result of my childhood. I bear full responsibility for my actions. I am only suggesting that the choices I made were somewhat influenced by the people and circumstances around which I grew up. Most of my decisions were made without much conscious thought. I believe that we all make choices or react to situations based on our past experiences and current circumstances without really thinking about them.

I am very grateful for the childhood I had, my family, my hometown and most of the things that happened to me growing up. I can't in any way blame any of those to justify my offense. I alone am responsible for what I did. I'm a **REGISTERED SEX OFFENDER FOR LIFE**.

So what possible credibility could I have that you would be interested in what I have to say? After all, I **AM** a convicted *sex offender*! Before you burn this book or regret that you bought it, I challenge you to read on as you may be more like me than you think. For some of you that could be very scary.

I decided to share my story with you so what happened in my life may not repeat itself in yours negatively affecting those you know and love. Later I'll get into who I victimized and try to unravel the reasons behind what moved me to behave in such a way. For now I ask you to open your eyes and mind to look beyond the OFFENDER and explore with me as I attempt to convey what went on. For some of you this might become uncomfortable. If it does, then my hope is that you find something in here that may alter the way you approach and make choices in your own life. You might even have the courage to explore the motives behind your choices that could ultimately lead to similar destructive consequences. I will share with you my life leading up to my offense, my prosecution, the outcome and the challenges that I face today as well as the way the public sees offenders and their role or exclusion in society.

Please take a moment before you read on. Think about your feelings and opinions regarding *SEX OFFENDERS.* Okay. Are you in touch with your biases? Do you think offenders are a lower class of people? Are you pissed? Disgusted? Are you suspect? Do you think I'm manipulating you? What if I am? Do you think you're big enough to handle this? Well, try to set all that aside and open your mind *for now the story begins.*

2

My defense attorney at the time of my trial had an interesting saying about most defendants. He said, "The difference between the criminals and the rest of us is that we all know where the line is. Some of us choose NOT to cross it. Not that we don't think about it." My brother-in-law told me, "We're all a little twisted. Some of the things that go on in my mind would scare the shit out of Steven King but I wouldn't DO it." (Come on, you've thought about some crap you're not proud of. You just haven't acted on it or have you and you just haven't been caught?) Once I asked him how he found the courage to defend criminals in court with a clear conscience. He told me in order to effectively do his job; he preferred to not actually know if an accused was guilty. He just knew that "at the end of the day, at least one of us was going to walk outta here."

(Gulp! Not a lot of real assurance for me at the time.)

The last week before my graduation from high school, my father took me down to the Railroad office (remember he was a railroad engineer) to introduce me to the Trainmaster and get me hired for what I thought was the summer. He showed up at my high school and found me goofing around during "water-balloon/squirt gun week." He said, "The party's over kid. It's time to go to work." As it turned out, one had to be eighteen and a high school graduate to get hired on the railroad. That was a problem because I was a month away from my eighteenth birthday. So his fatherly advice to me was to simply lie a little about my age by telling me to "Make a six (I was born in June) sort of look like a five (May) on the application." And he said it would take them more than a week to check on my graduation (they didn't have computers back then). By the time they got around to it I'd have my diploma anyway. He assured me it would be no big deal and a little **secret** between just the two of us.

I had very few special moments alone with my father when I was growing up because his job kept him "on the road." And I had four brothers and a sister to compete for his attention when he was home. So a job at the railroad would be a **BIG deal.** I wanted him to be proud of me for following in his footsteps. Looking back now I see that taking me to that office was his way of helping me become a man. He wanted me to get a "good union job" and told me he wasn't able to help me go to college. I did exactly as he advised and was hired immediately.

That was the first time I remember actually knowing I'd done something to please him. Bending the rules a little was no big deal. Right? So the lesson I learned was bending the rules just a little or telling a small lie and keeping it a secret was okay, in fact it was preferred, to get ahead. Today I'm sixty years old. This is the first time I've actually shared this particular incident with anyone.

I no longer work for the Railroad. My father has passed away. I'm qualified for benefits with the Railroad Retirement Board. I've decided to be a little more honorable and apply for them when I'm **actually** sixty-two instead of a month earlier because of that little lie that still remains on the record today.

I learned many lessons from my father as we all do. Even though he meant well, that was not a particularly good one. It is just a small example of the "sins" being passed on, a small portion of what would turn out to be a larger multi-generational "**curse.**" I learned that it was okay to manipulate things *just a little* for my own purposes, that the rules 'don't apply to me.' These "skills" and many others survived well into my adult life and, when practiced enough times, brought unbelievable hurt and devastation to the ones I love the most. My dad meant well, but just think about this. If it was okay to lie *a little*, bend the rule *a little,* then driving over the speed limit just *a little*, swiping a piece of candy at the store or some coins that weren't mine or cheating on a test or my taxes *just a little* was okay, too. Right?

My dad had the personality and sensitivity (or lack of it) of TV's Archie Bunker. He could watch **All in the Family** and not get it. He seriously didn't understand why everyone was laughing while we kids thought we were watching home movies complete with all the same bigotry, cynicism and attitudes. Sadly he treated my mom like Archie treated Edith. He showed no outward signs of affection in our presence. He expected her to serve him and respect him for providing for our family. Our home was HIS domain. HE was in command. I know that he cared for and protected us. He would have gotten after anyone that threatened us. But he was seemingly unable to express himself. He died, when I was thirty-four. He had never seen me in a sports contest or even in a uniform. I had never heard him say that he loved me, my mother or my siblings or that he was proud of any of us.

Dad retired early from the railroad around age sixty due to health reasons. During his last few working years we had a pretty good relationship, considering by that time I had become one of his Railroad supervisors. The tools, the love, the encouragement and the support that I should have gotten from a nurturing father I just didn't get. But I love and forgive my dad for his short-comings and don't blame him in any way for my actions. I accept that he was a flawed man like most of us, doing his best while enduring things that happened in his own life. I'll always respect his service to our country. He was a true hero in that respect.

As you read this book pay particularly close attention to the choices I made. I hope can see how very easy it was for me to miss the 'red flags.' See if you may be missing similar warnings in your own life. You might even review how you make your choices and avoid devastating mistakes. Now I invite you to explore with me the events in my life that caused me to realize the consequences of being **REGISTERED FOR LIFE**.

3

I graduated from high school and got my diploma (nobody ever checked). I thought I was well on my way to the "American Dream."

During the first few years after high school I continued to work on the railroad at a seniority based job. After the summer business slowed down I was laid off throughout the fall and winter. I took advantage of the time to take classes at a nearby Community College. It was the height of the Vietnam War and going to school allowed me to stay draft-deferred (kept me out of the military) as long as I maintained decent grades.

Several years later when my student deferment ran out, the military changed its draft procedure to a lottery system[3] by assigning a random number between 1 and 366 (to include those born on Feb. 29th) to each date of the calendar year. It then ranked those dates (birthdays) in numerical order to fill the draft requirement. The morning following that year's

---

[3]   Draft Lottery, www.sss.gov/lotter1.htm,

lottery (before there was an internet) I got up, dressed and went over to my parents' house. Together we opened the Saturday morning paper to see if I was in the top group. I had already decided to enlist the following Monday if my number was in the first 150 (lower numbers were drafted first). My number was 346. The dates right before and right after my birthday were both in the top ten! The following year the draft ended (and the Vietnam War)[4]. I continued to work and go to school. I did not serve in the military. I thought the Marine would have been disappointed that I hadn't volunteered. Instead he told me he thought Vietnam was some "real bullshit" and offered to help me avoid becoming a part of it. He never mentioned any details. I still don't know exactly what he meant.

During the months I was off the railroad and going to school I worked in construction for a local contractor I met at church. I learned many valuable trade skills from Bill. In fact, I probably should have been paying **him** for my "education." Three years later, still working my "summer job" at the railroad, I built my own first house (with Bill's help). There I was. All graduated from high school, working a union job, driving

---

[4] End of the Draft Lottery, landscaper.net/draft70-72.htm

a new car and an old pickup and building a three bedroom house. Might as well keep the "American Dream" going and get the wife and two and a half kids.

I met my first wife Nancy at college. She was there to get her MRS. degree (looking for a husband). I was there to maintain my student deferment. Only **one** of us "graduated." It was the beginning of a tragedy that lasted nearly twenty years. I entered adulthood optimistically thinking I was ready for the "Dream." In reality I was neither prepared to choose a mate nor start a family. My role model was Archie. My hormones ran rampant. I was twenty-one and, like most twenty-one year olds, didn't seek relationship advice. Confident and naïve, *I dove right in.*

Nancy was the third child of four being raised solely by her mother. Her parents divorced when she was four years old. Her father remained in the Mid-west when her mother brought the kids to California to be near their grandparents. Nancy, her older brother, older sister and younger brother were unsupervised growing up. Her mother was a nurse at a convalescent hospital across the street from their house. She worked the graveyard shift leaving the kids home alone during the night and she slept during the day.

Her father, while her parents were still together, was an alcoholic who abused all of them. Repeatedly he beat their mother right in front of the kids. He was also suspected of molesting them, too. But he passed away (via suicide) before that was ever verified.

When I met Nancy I didn't know how extensive her abuse had been. When she was *nine years* old she became the incest victim of her *sixteen year* old brother. She suffered various forms of his many sexual assaults, including intercourse (or more accurately rape), for four years. Then he enlisted in the Navy. That continuous abuse terrorized and enraged her. But her anger wasn't limited to her older brother. Her sister was four years older, big enough to tell him **NO** and fight him off of her. She did **nothing** to help her little sister. Her mother, whose memories of her own past abuse were "triggered" by Nancy's complaints, refused to believe her. She was so entrenched in her own denial that she wasn't "healthy" enough to protect her own daughter. Nancy was *devastated*. The abuse was allowed to continue unchecked. When she sought any assistance from anyone, the physical and sexual abuse she endured from her brother only worsened. Even when he was home "on leave" from the Navy he still tried to 'do things' to Nancy. By then, though, she was in her teens and able, with some effort, to fend him off herself.

When all the abuse was disclosed to me I, too, was devastated. After the initial shock, I felt it my husbandly duty to get her professional help. (I also wanted a big piece of her brother's hide). My hope was if we found a trusted counselor she would "open up" and reveal the horrific trauma she had endured as a child. She would have someone who could guide her through her "emotional minefield." I hoped given enough time with such support she would eventually "heal."

But the deeply seeded pain and fury made raging her "comfort zone". When she was angry at anything she screamed uncontrollably. I was her favorite target and suffered many verbal and physical assaults. **Nothing** was off limits. Being inexperienced and still adjusting to married life, I failed to consider that all that rage might be attributed to her *incestuous abuse*. I thought she was just mad at me or unhappy with our circumstances.

My lesson by example of the Marine had been to "handle it." So I tried harder to please her. No matter what I did she wasn't content. I was so unprepared for such a challenge! Finally I realized that for the first time in her life I had provided the only real measure of safety for her to "let it all out". She had **a lot** to unload. I felt I was strong and could absorb her tantrums as long as I didn't take it personally. If I had helped her vent that was good. Right? To me it was like unplugging a clogged drain. Once the blockage had been removed everything ran smoothly down the pipe. I *was so naïve*. I hadn't grasped that her abusive past had been a "generator". She couldn't be just unplugged and everything didn't run smoothly. She remained blocked.

One of my dad's many sayings is "A steady drip of water running long enough will wear a hole through a granite boulder." Her "dripping" never ceased. As time went on, patterns emerged. When she raged I'd just let her go and would try to avoid her outburst. I noticed if I didn't engage her while she "blew off some steam" she seemed to get over it faster and calm down. After a day or so, she would be remorseful regretting she had taken so much liberty with her assaults. Occasionally she was even apologetic. But that didn't solve anything. I still "stuffed" **my** feelings.

Many years later after we divorced I asked her, "When did I give you permission to yell at me and call me names?" She was startled by my question. I'm amazed at the way people in relationships act towards one another. At what time during a developing relationship, does it become okay to shout foul names at each other with a total lack of respect? At what point in "falling in love" do we start assuming we have gained the right to be-little and condemn? We're supposed to love each other. Yet we behave worse towards those closest to us than we would in schools, our jobs, churches or any social setting.

She thought about what I had said and asked me for forgiveness. I accepted her apology. I forgave her. But let me tell you. Today I stay completely "off the firing range". Just in case.

All those years I acted as if her attacks never bothered me. But over time it took a heavy toll. Instead of taking care of and understanding my partner worthy of unconditional love, I treated her as a problem. Her raging caused me to defend myself emotionally. I set up a "perimeter" around my emotions to safeguard my inner self. I tried to limit my hurt and disappointment. Her past had caused her so much pain that she was unavailable to me as a wife. I was unable to share my feelings, fears and weaknesses with her. I could show no sign of being vulnerable or needy. I had to be consistently strong in our relationship. Even when we shared intimate things, they weren't kept in confidence. When she raged out of my presence, she lost all control and divulged our deepest, most private moments with her friends. I couldn't trust my wife. I could not be emotionally safe around her. Think about that!

Have you ever found yourself yelling at the one you're supposed to love the most only to be interrupted by the phone and calmly and politely answer it? Most of us would never conduct ourselves that way around strangers or in public. We seem to have adopted a different set of rules for our most cherished relationships.

During the second winter of our marriage the railroad transferred me to a suburb of Sacramento. We sold the home I had built and moved. I looked forward to living a couple of hours' drive from Nancy's family. I was especially eager to get away from her older brother. He was a few years older than I and arrogant and intimidating. By that time he had been discharged from the Navy, was married with a family and (the ultimate of irony) was a *cop* in our small town. (To this very day, some forty years later, he has never accepted any responsibility for his incestuous actions. He still refuses to even speak of them.) I hoped that moving would distance her from her childhood torture. However, her scars were so deeply embedded that moving away didn't alleviate anything. During our home sale and move Nancy was pregnant with our first child. So the burden of moving was solely on me. I solicited the help of one of my brothers and we did the old 'rent a truck and move ourselves' thing.

There has been no greater joy in my life than I felt becoming a father for the first time. Shelly came into our life on the 8th day of the 8th month of 1975 (my 24th year). She was the most beautiful baby I'd ever seen. I was glowing. I was a very proud father. Becoming a parent changed everything. I recall driving Nancy and our baby home from the hospital on a cool summer morning determined to give Shelly a much more nurturing father than mine had been to me. I told Nancy we were bringing our child home to **our** house. Not the other way around! We weren't going to let her run things and take over. We were going to provide proper structure, discipline, lots of love and a safe warm home. She would learn that she was loved and to respect us. We were going to give her opportunities to develop her dreams and reach her goals. We were setting rules, boundaries and limitations that she may grow up feeling secure and confident. I hadn't realized how ill prepared I was for the task. I already had my hands full being a husband to a wife with many needs far beyond my understanding, much less my ability to fulfill.

Generally we were feeling pretty good about our station in life. We were in our mid-twenties. I was getting steady work at the railroad. We had our home and the responsibility of being parents. Two years later we were blessed with our son Mark, born 11/11/77. (How's that for a lucky number?) Two years after that our second daughter Ann (6/27/79) completed our family. So there it is. Our two and a half kids. The 'American Dream'. We laugh to this day about which one is the half. When people asked me, "How many children do you have?" I said, "We have three. One of each." That pissed them all off.

Nancy and I set about raising our kids. I was a taking all the overtime and extra days I could get so Nancy could be a stay-at-home Mom. By the time all the kids were finally in school we'd settled into a kind of cruise control except for Nancy's "issues." I don't mean to sound insensitive. They were truly deep and very painful. But years had passed and therapy didn't seem to have any impact. It became increasingly clear to me that she probably never would completely resolve her past enough to move forward. I can't know the level of destruction her incestuous abuse caused. But I was hoping at some point the counseling and her *willingness* to face her demons would at least put some sort of limit on how it was running her life and affecting our relationship. She was absent as a parent to our children and as a wife to me.

Years later I learned from one of our adult children that she was eventually diagnosed as having bipolar disorder. That made a lot of sense to me. While we were married one day she was hysterical and throwing a fit; the next she acted as if nothing had happened. I never imagined it could have been physiological. I saw myself as somewhat balanced. I saw her as an emotional roller coaster. My challenge was to figure out what part of the cycle she was in and proceed with caution.

I tried to behave calmly and *steady the ship.* I knew that in a day or two that particular incident would blow over. We would continue on until the next one. I was never aware that Nancy saw that as indifference which only frustrated her further. As a result, I spent most of my energy taking care of my wife and the kids and not paying much attention to myself. That really wore down my battery. I felt like I was living with *four* kids. I resented the burden. I was disheartened and embittered. I felt I'd been cheated by not having a wife in whom I could confide. I received no encouragement and rarely any gratitude. I shut down emotionally.

If you are married or in a relationship and you cannot be vulnerable and share your deepest feelings for fear of being ridiculed, you are in deep trouble, my friend. Your needs are not being met.

4

During my senior year of high school some of my friends introduced me to a "Youth for Christ" outreach program called Campus Life[5]. While growing up I had little exposure to "church". Campus Life was a way to satisfy my curiosity about spiritual things. It was a place for young people like me to have some wholesome fun, make new friends and talk about things on their minds. They accepted me without any conditions. I didn't have to act. I could just be a kid. It was a safe place to talk. It provided me life skills I would need to live in this turbulent world. I attended their "impact" events that were usually parties or focused gatherings. Later I went to "insight" meetings, usually informal and held at someone's house. I learned basic Christian beliefs. I have fond memories of barbecues and swim parties followed by a few words of "insight" to let you know they cared about you. In the fall of my senior year on the 30th of October 1968, in the front seat of a 1967 Olds 442 parked in the lot of a Safeway store, I accepted

---

[5] Campus Life, www.yfc.net/campuslife/

Jesus Christ into my life. I continue to have a relationship with Him today. He NEVER fails. I certainly haven't always *followed* him. But I have never stopped *believing* in Him.

When our kids were little, we attended church on a regular basis. We thought church should be a part of their childhoods that ours had lacked. I became involved in church leadership and taught high school and adult Sunday school classes. Nancy was in the choir. Our "church family" became very meaningful to us socially. There were many occasions when we were invited to friends' homes or hosted a gathering at our house. I became friends with the pastor and some of the men.

My wife was constantly needy, always taking and returning nothing. I became increasingly disillusioned with my marriage. I began relying on friends as an escape from my situation. Most of my spare time was involved with church activities or friends. Nancy resented that and understandably felt neglected. So she constantly called around town (before there were pagers or cell phones) wanting to know where I was, who I was with, what I was doing and, most importantly, when was I coming home. Our relationship was in turmoil. I'm sure I failed her as much as I felt she had failed me.

We had no answers. I felt alone and conflicted between my belief in honoring my commitment to stay and leaving what was becoming a miserable marriage. We were living together but we were emotionally isolated. She was consumed by her "issues". I felt abandoned, lonely and empty.

I tried to share my feelings with my few friends including my pastor. Their consistent advice was to "stick it out," to hang in there at all cost. My pastor said the promise of my marriage vow was between not only my wife and I but also with God. He described it like a triangle with God holding two of the sides. "You don't want to go against God, do you?" Our congregation was small, primarily twenty-to-thirty-year-old couples. Most had young children. The idea of divorce, even mentioning the "**D**" word was like unleashing a deadly disease. It was understood a **spiritual** man would hang in there if for no other reason than to honor God.

Fortunately for me that was some thirty years ago. I've grown and changed considerably since those days. I don't accept that kind of guilty conservative view as much as I did in my idealistic youth. I sometimes think it is easy for "church" people to give canned advice without thinking. Those "church" people wouldn't even know what I was talking about if I brought up such things as "judging others" or "gluttony" at a church pot-luck.

Nancy and I had lost total emotional trust in each other and all ability to communicate. Nancy, bound by her past, was constantly in a state of chaos. I ignored my feelings and focused on taking care of the family, being a dad. After all, our children had a right to a nurturing childhood. Little did I know that was just setting us up for more problems down the road.

Managing our finances was about as successful as our marriage. The kind of work I was doing at the railroad meant my earnings varied from payday to payday. But in the summer of 1983 I had the opportunity to consider a transfer to Tucson, Arizona thereby increasing my earnings about 40% annually.

Since the beginning of our marriage Nancy had a desire to return to school. She took classes at the local junior college when she wasn't attending counseling. I'm certainly not knocking an education. But she had established a track record of beginning classes every semester and dropping most of them before it ended. I viewed that as a complete waste of time and neglect of our children. I felt like she was going to school for her own self-esteem as a social outlet. To me she was using college to "escape" being a mom rather than having a purpose like completing a degree for a career when kids were older. I resented her for having the freedom and flexibility to take classes and when it got a little tough, she could drop out. As a husband and father I didn't have that option. I was making it possible for her to go to school *and* get counseling. I figured if she was smart enough to grasp higher education subjects it was her deliberate choice not to take the counseling seriously and work to resolve her issues". The reason that I bring up her education is because I resented her being "damaged". I concluded she was either *unwilling* to face her pain or *unable* to limit the effects of her past abuse to be in the present as my wife. I admit that I was pretty narrow-minded. I was focused on *her* and *her* problems which irritated the hell out of me. All that resentment started a terminal cancer in our relationship. I wasn't happy. I was miserable and the worst part was that I knew it. I made the choice to stay in the marriage. I decided it was just my "curse".

Years later I had a friend tell me following her divorce, she elected to remain single even though at times it was tremendously lonely. "It sure beats the crap out of constantly being miserable," she said.

Nancy and I discussed moving to Tucson. It went about as well as everything else we'd tried to discuss. She resisted the idea. I told her I could earn much more money there, eliminate all our bills, have better lives and provide more opportunities for our children. I also promised her she could attend the University of Arizona. She finally agreed to move.

We put our house up for sale and started packing. Nancy and I discussed what we wanted in a home there. Then I made an advance trip alone to Tucson to lease one. That would give us plenty of time to become familiar with the different areas before we "settled in" and bought one. Our track-sized home in Sacramento was crowded with three growing kids. We were hoping to find a larger house that each of our kids could have his/her own room. The house I found was enormous! It was about twice the square footage of our Sacramento home and had all the bedrooms we needed. It also had an office, family room and separate living room plus an inside laundry. In the finished back yard was a built-in heated pool.

The railroad made a "free" boxcar available to us for the move. It was large enough to hold all our household belongings and my pickup too. We packed and took a few days loading it.

The children were really excited about getting their own rooms and a pool. It was *their* first move and quite an adventure.

We left the Sacramento area and traveled south towards Tucson. Everything we owned was in that boxcar except for what we would take on vacation in suitcases. We knew the railroad would take four or five days longer to get "our" boxcar to Tucson than it would take us driving. So we planned a few days at Disneyland. Ann was starting into kindergarten, Mark the second grade and Shelly the fourth. We had a terrific time! We finally made it to Tucson dead tired from our "vacation." When our things had also arrived we set up our new home. Then school began.

I had been a Yardmaster which was a supervisory position with the railroad in Sacramento. By electing to go to Tucson I had to resign my supervisory status and return to a seniority system which put me back working on the trains. (That would prove to be a significant decision later). I started back as a freight conductor traveling on trains either between Tucson and Yuma, Arizona or Tucson and Lordsburg, New Mexico for days at a time. Nancy became impatient and wanted to return to school right away. We had discussed her taking a year off or at most taking a few transferable classes at the community college that first year to avoid paying a much higher tuition as she was then considered an "out of state" student. The residency requirement for the University's "in state" tuition required living in the State at least one year. But she insisted and since I had promised, she became UA's new "out of state" student. I paid. She went. And of course she dropped out as usual. I was pissed.

The following spring we chose an area on the east side of town and made arrangements to purchase a new home being built by a developer. Our financial picture was getting brighter. I was earning at a much better pace than even I had anticipated before the move. So in addition to buying a new home for our family we also bought a nearby rental. That property was a "fixer upper" in need of significant upgrades. I was working on the railroad and spending my "off" time getting it ready for the tenants we had promised it to by a certain date. It was the last part of May. The school year had almost ended. The kids were looking forward to the summer spending time with their new friends, sleeping-in and swimming in the pool. I had scheduled a few weeks vacation. All of us were going to put the finishing touches on the rental house and move into our new home.

Nancy had other plans. Since we weren't communicating (or I wasn't listening) I didn't have a clue how much she hated the desert and was homesick for Sacramento. Without any warning, she loaded the kids in the car on the last day of school and took off to California. I was away on a train run. When I got home I didn't know whether she was mad at me, our situation, her painful past or missing "home." All I knew was that I had been *abandoned* and left with all the responsibility of moving into our new home and meeting the rental deadline for our tenants. I worked my butt off the entire following week. At the last possible moment I learned she had informed the new tenants we were GETTING A DIVORCE! She had advised them not to move in. THEY knew we were getting divorced before I did! I was shocked, tired and furious. I was worn out and overwhelmed. I mean totally exhausted physically *and* emotionally. My family was gone. I still had a week left of vacation. I got on a plane, flew to Sacramento and rented a car. You might be thinking I was going after my wife and kids to bring them back and fix everything. Not even close.

5

As I shared with you earlier, I had a pretty good childhood growing up in a small town. We had only one high school and I was blessed to have some good friends there. It was the mid-sixties. We had Friday night football or basketball games followed by dances and, of course, our muscle cars. My buddies and I would take our girlfriends home at midnight when the dances ended and meet out in the country. We'd race our cars until either the sun showed up or the cops did. Those days were much like the movie "American Graffiti.[6]" In fact, the movie was made about Modesto, CA which was a short drive away. Anyway, I had a special friend, Alyssa. She was not like any of my girlfriends. She was a *real* friend. She was the one I'd hang out with when neither of us had a date. I was always welcomed anytime at her family's home. She had one little sister and no brothers. Her dad was cool. He took an interest in me. And her little Italian mom could cook! Mama Mia! They were a working class family like my own.

---

[6] American Graffiti, wikipedia.org/wiki/American_Graffiti

Their home was comfortable. I didn't have to put up a front or try to impress her or her parents. Alyssa and I spent many hours contemplating life, dreaming of the future, sharing our souls and being friends (when we weren't driving my dad's jeep through the rock quarry or off-roading in the nearby foothills). I respected her. Simple as that. I never kissed her or dated her like my girlfriends. We didn't go out except for two times as default dates cause we didn't have a real date. It's very interesting to me after all these years I still remember the details of our "not dates" much more vividly than any of the real dates with my girlfriends back then. Remember the "Marine" said, "The party is over kid." I went to work. Alyssa went to Southern California (USC)[7]. We lost touch and that was too bad for both of us.

The car I rented was a fast Mustang (not your typical family car). I had forgotten the feeling of freedom driving a "hot" car down the freeway with the windows open and fresh air blowing in my face, radio blaring. I drove straight to Alyssa's. I hadn't seen her in over ten years. But we had written a few times and I was aware of her circumstances. She was a divorced single mother living about an hour south of Sacramento with her ten

---

[7] USC, University of Southern California, www.usc.edu/

year old son, Adam. She had recently completed her education and an internship while raising Adam by herself. I had helped her out a few times when she was struggling to make ends meet. She never asked me for help. But I knew her well enough to know that she needed it. When I contacted her she was home recovering from foot surgery. She invited me to come see her.

I needed Alyssa. I needed my **friend**. I needed that friend who knew me way back when and didn't judge me. She loved me. I don't mean she was "in love" with me. But she loved me in a *best friend* way. She was like a cold glass of water on a scorching hot day. She respected my marriage and encouraged me to take time, get myself together and deal with things. She offered me a comforting, safe place to relax. Something only **real** friends do. She understood and appreciated me. I was grateful to have her.

Alyssa gave me some much needed validation. She told me everything I did wasn't crap. She told me I was a good father. She helped me regain my sense of worth. She encouraged me to return to Nancy and the kids to "work it out" or be sure about "breaking up." Her allowing me a calm and restful place to recharge myself, I was able to muster enough strength to gather my little children at my mother's house (nearby) to tell them that Mommy and Daddy were getting a divorce. There just isn't any good way to tell your children that. I held them, tried to soothe them and assured them that things would be okay. Their mom and I each loved them. We just couldn't be together anymore. Up to that point in my life, it was the toughest thing I had ever faced. There would be more to confront. I'll get to that later.

I had a few remaining days of my vacation and asked Alyssa, "When was the last time you were on a *real* vacation." She laughed and said, "Vacation! I'm lucky to have enough extra money for a pizza much less a vacation!" So I took her and Adam to Monterey on the Pacific coast. We went to the Aquarium and the beaches and real restaurants that didn't have a drive-thru. We did the Cannery Row[8] thing and enjoyed ourselves. We laughed, relaxed and let loose. We loved each other but were not *lovers*. It was so refreshing! To this day she's grateful for the time we spent there and for the joy I brought to her and her son. I was grateful for my **true** friend and got my battery charged for what was to come.

I soon returned to Tucson alone and went back to work. I was a conductor riding on the trains. But soon I was becoming

---

[8] Cannery Row, caviews.com/can.htm

a *train wreck*. I got an attorney and filed for divorce. After all my wife had left me! During the next couple of weeks or months, it sort of runs together, I flew Alyssa and Adam to Tucson for a visit. We spent a few days together. Then they returned to California. It was a "big deal" for them. I think it was Adam's first plane trip. I went about trying to salvage the properties. It became a lost cause. So did I.

I felt I couldn't stay in Tucson and continue to work for a number of reasons. I missed my kids and I didn't like myself enough to live alone. I had an empty feeling that I thought only being in a relationship would fill.

Alyssa had nearly recovered from her foot rehab and was looking to change her career path. It had been a struggle raising a child alone, finishing her college degree, passing her State Board medical license test and completing an internship as a Medical Technologist in a local hospital. She told me her heart's desire was a career in medical marketing. The best opportunity to pursue that was in Orange County, Southern California, a more corporate environment. I considered my situation and proposed that I move her and Adam there. I could just transfer to L.A. with the railroad. We leased a place together and moved.

6

During the previous winter I had the pleasure of spending what would become the last Christmas with my father. He was forced to retire from the railroad after thirty-five years due to medical reasons. He had moved to the southern part of Idaho to enjoy his retirement years living near the places he had previously visited on past vacations. (I neglected to tell you that my parents divorced when I was twenty-six. He then married his last wife, Roberta). I recall with pleasure that during the time we spent together in Idaho my dad and I had a few of those "special" moments. We just sort of made eye contact and it was understood the torch was about to pass. He let me know he was proud of me and respected me as a man. I told him I was grateful to have him as a dad. That was the best it ever got between us. When I left him, I had a strange feeling I wouldn't understand until after he passed. A month or so later Roberta called to say my dad had an "event." He had lost touch with reality. He remained home approximately nine months before he passed. Roberta, a retired nurse, took very good care of him during that time. I am grateful he "lost touch" before Nancy and I separated. He was never aware of our problems.

I don't recall the details but somehow Nancy had managed to move our stuff (which magically became **her** stuff) back to the Sacramento area with what I suspected was help from our former church friends. I moved myself and the "two bags" she left me to Southern California to be with Alyssa and Adam.

The legal requirement was six months in the location of filing a divorce petition with the court. So I filed in Tucson to get it over with. We were given a court date the first part of September, four months after we had separated. I purchased a thirty day advance airline ticket.

Out court date was on a Thursday afternoon. I was at work on Tuesday afternoon of the same week when I got "the call." My dad had died. I was stunned. There is no way to avoid the pain of losing a loved one, especially a parent. I had never experienced losing anyone in my immediate family. The timing couldn't have been worse! I was used to certain kinds of pain but that was different. Alyssa was there for me and comforted me in my grief. She was wonderful and understanding. I was sad, distraught and grieved the next two days. Sobbing at times, laughing about good memories, then more tears, emptiness and loss. But somehow I found the strength to leave for Tucson and face *divorce court*. In retrospect I probably could have gotten our court date changed. But I wanted to get the mess behind me.

My father's funeral was scheduled for the next morning (Friday) in Idaho. Thursday morning I left L.A. and flew to Tucson and went straight to my attorney's office. In the same building was a travel agency. Hurrying to make court, I went into the agency and left my credit card with instructions to book a flight that evening to Salt Lake City. I asked them to have a car reserved for me at the airport when I landed so I could drive to Idaho in time for my dad's memorial service in the morning.

Court was a drain. The judge ruled that I was responsible for all our debt and support for the kids and gave custody to Nancy (the so called caregiver). The proceedings lasted beyond the business hours of the travel agency. When I returned to retrieve my ticket to attend my fathers' funeral I was met with an envelope taped outside the door. It contained my credit card and a note saying the airline charges didn't clear. THERE WAS NO TICKET TO SALT LAKE CITY. I was devastated. I had no other options. My "Ex" still being on all of my credit cards had cancelled them. I was stuck trying to arrange transportation to attend my own father's memorial service and running out of time. All of my siblings were already in route to Idaho and unable to be contacted (there were no cell phones back then). I boarded the plane in Tucson using my return ticket. Sadly instead of going to Salt Lake City as planned, I had no choice but to return to L.A. I was the only child of the six of us that wasn't at our father's funeral. I felt ashamed. Later I apologized to my siblings for allowing my circumstances to prevent me from attending.

In the following months, Alyssa and I set about creating a life for ourselves and Adam in Southern California. She searched for a job. I worked all I could to support us as well as my own children. The holidays were approaching. I hadn't seen my children in nearly six months. I missed them very much. I had times when I would just be overcome with emotion and cry feeling the loss of not being around my precious little kids. Finally, I couldn't stand being away from them any longer. Alyssa cautioned me to be patient and together we would plan a trip for me to see them. I was impatient. I left by myself and headed north. The drive from L.A. to Sacramento was about eight hours. The closer I got the more excited I became to see my kids.

I arrived in the afternoon at the apartment where they were living. We hugged. We cried. It was very emotional. They were so happy to see me and I them. It felt like a momentary healing from nagging loss filling my empty heart with a little joy. For them a sense that everything was ok if only for a short time. I was in no state of mind to make any clear decisions regarding anything.

Nancy informed our "church friends" and Pastor that I was in town. They welcomed me like the prodigal husband/father returning from having *sinned*. Nancy wanted me back. The kids wanted me back. My former church friends wanted me to come back and care for my family. I was *surrounded*. They had put a pretty convincing guilt trip on me. They seemed to want us to "patch" things up. But none cared enough to understand our relationship could not be fixed with a "patch" if at all.

Nancy still clung to her "issues." By then they had become a sort of badge of courage. She played the victim card well and got tons of sympathy from the whole group. Being back in the old "church family" empowered her and placed the cause of all our "problems" on me. I was out-gunned and out-numbered. I was too raw and vulnerable to defend myself. I *caved*. I decided to return to them which placed me right back in the 'blender' with Nancy. I was still ignorant of so much.

The Pastor and Gary, another church member, accompanied me back to L.A. to walk out on Alyssa and her son, get my stuff and return 'home.' I was such a wimp that I brought Alyssa's parents into the mix by having them be in L.A. to soften the blow to her of my leaving. I knew she didn't have anybody there and her parents would help her arrange to move on. I even gave her father some money for their relocation expenses thinking I was doing something honorable.

So in just six months I had inflicted a lot of pain. On my children by abandoning them to be in L.A. Then abandoning Alyssa and Adam without any notice, leaving just when the boy, had for the first time in his life, a "Daddy." I regret I behaved in such a cowardly and hurtful manner.

I returned to Sacramento with the Pastor and Gary. Everyone in the church rejoiced. I was humbled, humiliated and, for the first time in my life, ashamed. I was reminded it was God's will for me to be back. He would heal our relationship and provide for my family.

You will recall I have had a relationship with Jesus since I was a teenager. At that time though, I can best describe the relationship as if I was driving down the highway of life with Jesus in the car but not as a passenger, driver or navigator, rather as a spare tire or a first-aid kit in the trunk, in case of an emergency. Once in a while I'd stop to check to make sure I had my "supplies." I felt God was my personal "bellhop" in the sky. He was just waiting to jump at my every wish. God's healing wasn't going to happen. The relationship "cancer" was only in remission. Returning was the beginning of what would set in motion more tragic events with more terrible consequences.

7

Returning to Sacramento and Nancy and my kids, I had to deal with the consequences of my decision. I had devastated my *real* friend and her son by leaving them in L.A. without warning or even a discussion.

Looking back I realize the Pastor and Gary hadn't gone all that way just to help me pack. More importantly to them in the event I wavered in my decision or actually followed my heart and not leave Alyssa, they would intervene and **bring** me back.

I thought I was returning "for the sake of the kids." My advice for anyone trying to stay together "for the sake of the kids" is to get out and get help. I know that's easier said than done. But I was ignorant of the support available to me to continue to be a good father apart from resuming and enduring that doomed relationship with Nancy. From the beginning, I had taken my marriage vows and my commitment as a dad seriously. I let my low self esteem, guilt, shame and the pressure of my "friends" cloud my ability to realize I had options. I let those feelings become part of my "curse." I'm sure my 'friends' meant well. I don't have an issue with what they did. But they didn't have a clue about the disease growing within my marriage. The entire church's mentality seemed black and white. Preserve marriage at all cost. Such a rigid inflexible position lacked any tolerance, understanding or compassion.

It was years later I found out what happened to Alyssa. The very next day after I left her, she had pulled herself together for a job interview. She was extended an offer and with the help of her parents moved to the San Francisco Bay area. She started a new career in medical marketing.

Another consequence of my decision to return to Nancy was I withdrew the divorce petition in Tucson. The court rulings had been only temporary. The final date had not arrived. At the time none of my 'friends' or even my paid attorney reminded me that I had been the one **abandoned.** How dare she take the kids and flee the state (Arizona)! No matter what the problem had been Tucson was where **we** decided to live. It was where our family home was and I made a living for our family. But true to my pattern of being Nancy's caretaker, I turned away from Alyssa, my peace and happiness and followed Nancy back to Sacramento "for the kid's sake." Instead I should have said to Nancy, "If you want to be together get your ass and our kids back to Tucson!"

Lastly, for me to return indirectly meant I could no longer work for the railroad. I shared with you earlier that in order to move I had to resign in Sacramento my supervisory position to work a seniority job in Tucson. There weren't any positions available in Sacramento for my seniority level. The railroad was down-sizing and offered a "buy-out" or severance package to any employee who voluntarily left. Since they were willing to pay me not to be there, it was probably time to move on. I resigned after more than seventeen years with them and began looking for work. I didn't realize how much of my identity and self-worth I had derived from my job until I was absent from it.

The severance package didn't last long.

Nancy had gotten a job with the State of California. I was scrounging for anything I could get, miscellaneous construction jobs and handyman work. Our relationship continued to deteriorate. We had serious money problems and eventually declared bankruptcy. We lost our real estate in Arizona. We were renting in Sacramento. (That was worse than when I was single! At least THEN I owned my own home.) My self esteem plummeted. The power balance in our marriage had shifted. She had a steady job. I was out of work most of the time and felt *helpless*. Nancy was getting all kinds of moral support from the church. She had the "he left me for another woman" (instead of he left me because I'm fucking crazy) victim card in her arsenal to pull out any time it was convenient to club me. She became a pro.

I went back to church but was never really embraced nor forgiven by many. I was deemed "inappropriate" for leadership or teaching. I was relegated to second class status (the Scarlet Letter syndrome). My "friends" kept me at a distance. I was no longer invited to their homes. Not only had I cheated but I also couldn't keep my wife "in-line." After what he did, who could blame her? We needed their compassion. We were kept at arms length. I needed their love and understanding. I received their scorn and neglect. Nancy needed more than any church could offer.

Generally, I believe most churches are very skilled at "killing their wounded" instead of helping them heal. (Mine certainly was.) I don't mean to come down on churches for what they teach but rather on the people and how they act towards each other in spite of what they are taught and supposed to believe.

Today I actually have Jesus riding inside the car with me. On a good day, He drives. On an especially good day, I even follow where He leads me. Those days are the ones when I **know** I'm truly blessed. Then the smallest of things becomes awesome and I experience a glimpse of HIS peace and gain a sense of balance.

I was fortunate to have one remaining church friend, Jerry who was a building contractor. He had been an expert sniper in the Marine Corps during the Vietnam War and had certainly seen his share of suffering. He was a very compassionate man and offered me employment (over his wife's objections). For the next few years, we worked together. Then Jerry decided to quit the construction business altogether and return to school to complete his education. He went on to become a history teacher, his real "first love." But before he shut down his business, he helped me get a Contractor's license. Today I am a General Contractor operating my own construction business. I will always be grateful for Jerry and his generosity. He helped me provide for my family when it really counted.

So I was back "home" with my family out of work (before Jerry), had a wife filled with another load of things to be angry about and children turning into young adults. I had made some very bad decisions and scrambled things up pretty good. Nancy was more distant and angrier than ever. She had adapted well to "playing therapy" with her counselors. It was easier for her to focus on me and ignore her part of the problems than it was to work towards healing some of her deeply seeded pain. **I became the issue**. We were even less connected. We had no intimacy whatsoever. I didn't say sex. I said intimacy! Sex wasn't the problem. Communicating our inner selves was. We had no genuine love. We both let our resentment and pain separate us so far apart that we lost the very will to pull it back together. My unfulfilled emptiness became my CURSE. I told myself to "stay for my kids." I decided to stick it out.

8

In the fall of '87 the school year began like most had with the lazy days of summer and the kids sleeping in gone for another season. It had been a tumultuous few years with losing my dad, breaking up and then reconciling with Nancy and the involvement with and loss of Alyssa and Adam.

I had two major issues persistently nagging at me. First, Nancy was commuting to her new job and left earlier in the morning than the kids did for school. So I was trying to adapt to the awkward role of getting them up, dressed, fed and on their way. I also tried being around in the afternoon when they returned home earlier than she got off work. Secondly, we constantly argued about her full-time employment and my lack of any steady income. My inability to get sustainable work was an endless irritant on me in particular. Nancy staying true-to-form was always "at the ready" to point out how I needed to *get some work* along with the usual name calling and rage. I had enough of a challenge to keep myself focused on what I was trying to do. Then I'd try to handle her shot gunning verbal lambasting assaults at me being a *loser*. What a mess. I began applying for 'State' jobs to keep her off my back.

A morning routine had developed around our house. Nancy was the first one up to get ready to go to her job. I followed and got the kids up to start their day. Shelly was 12 and in the eighth grade, Mark was 10 and in sixth grade. Ann was 8 and in the fourth grade. The two younger kids left for school before Shelly did as they were in different schools at the time. Shelly was in junior high (middle school) and becoming a teenager. She was extremely bright and outgoing. Even then she seemed mature beyond her years. I began sharing some of my stress and frustration with her. Since her mom had "checked out", it was comforting to be able to talk about my problems without triggering a fit of rage. She challenged me intellectually. I saw her as a copy of her mother but UNDAMAGED. That should have been a **giant red flag.** But I was so empty and needy that I confided in her how carrying the responsibility of our family made me feel.

She was understanding and encouraging. The problem was it was not *her* role to listen to *my* problems. She was a teenager. She had a right to feel and act like one. Instead I talked to her as if she was my peer. I complemented her and trusted her beyond anything healthy, much less normal, as her dad. I was so caught up in my own stuff that I completely missed my kid's needs for a stable, protective father, especially Shelly's. This breakdown of the normal father-daughter boundaries mutated into a role shift. Shelly became the mother and Nancy, all caught up in her own stuff was behaving like one of the kids. It was refreshing. I looked forward to talking with Shelly. It was miserable to try to have a conversation with Nancy. That should have been another **big red flag**. I was too cowardly to genuinely look at myself. Unable to discover who I really was. What made me tick?

As I look back on it I realize that it was not a real *relationship* that I had with my oldest daughter. More accurately it was an *entrapment*. I had responded to my child's love by obscuring the parent-child boundaries. I had elevated her to the status of my surrogate partner to meet *my* emotional needs. I developed and encouraged an inappropriate bond with my child. I got my needs met at her expense and neglected what she needed. At some point, my relationship with Shelly became more important than my relationship with my wife. That was the point where Shelly became *psychologically* abused, a sort of *emotional incest*.

Meanwhile, Shelly had become Nancy's sounding board as well. I'm sure Nancy was frustrated at my being so insensitive and indifferent. My saturation limit had been reached. I turned a deaf ear towards any of her "stuff." So she reached out and depended on Shelly in her own way. We were both unable and unwilling to meet each other's needs. Instead we forced our neediness onto our daughter. Neither of us was even aware that we were both neglecting Shelly's real needs.

Imagine the pressure of hearing all that stuff from each of your parents having the responsibility of your younger brother and sister thrust upon you while going through puberty. What a recipe for crazy making! No wonder she became overwhelmed and hid in her room reading for hours to escape the chaos in our home. She ran away more than once, spent a short time in foster care and eventually emancipated herself as her only way out.

Throughout the school year as the morning routine developed, I started a habit of calling the kids into our master bedroom in the mornings having them cuddle or wrestle with me on the bed before getting ready for school. Nancy was rushing around always late trying to get out the door to work.

When she left, it was like a tornado had passed. A moment of calmness. Then Mark and Ann were next to finish readying themselves and went off to school. I would cuddle with Shelly until it was time for her to get ready to leave.

We really didn't have a lot of boundaries so I thought nothing of the kids being in my bed. I was still treating them as little kids. But they weren't so little anymore. Shelly was developing into a young woman. My behavior caused her to feel uncomfortable, to say the least. I'm sure she had her own concerns coping with changes to her body without me adding to them. I didn't know at the time that was the case but I certainly should have. Ignorantly I continued the morning routine.

My behavior was never initiated as a form of sexual gratification. I was never aroused by it. I felt connected and validated, neither of which I should have sought from my child. I thought I was showing and getting affection. Nothing more. Then things changed. I touched her chest. It happened on numerous occasions. I didn't put much stock in it at the time. I still don't even recall how often it happened. I was so out of touch with myself I was not aware of how sexual I was becoming. I'm sure that Shelly had an icky, creepy feeling about it. When I held her, I felt no tension from her (which was hardly the case with her mother). At first Shelly didn't seem to mind. But that began to change too. She resisted coming into my room at all.

It's unbelievable now when I think back at how I acted toward her. How utterly dysfunctional it was! I put the burden on my own child having to protect herself from her father's inappropriate acts. How was it that I could have robbed my child of a safe environment? One where she could be allowed to voice her own opinions, have her own ideas, become comfortable with changes in her body and be free from fearing **me**. I know now that I'm largely responsible for her "acting out" later having treated her that way. It was about to get worse.

The school year had passed by quickly. It was once again summer. I was doing some intermittent contract work for a commercial property management company in Sacramento. One of their clients owned a large apartment complex a hundred miles away which needed some balcony repairs. The work could only be done in the summer as that particular place was mostly student housing for a nearby State University. It was too far to commute and the job would take about three weeks to complete. I decided to travel there in two or three day increments spread over those three weeks balancing my time between work and home. The kids were out of school and summertime was a challenge for their mother and me to come up with things to occupy them. We decided I would take Shelly with me on one of my trips. She could see what kind of work I was doing and be exposed to the University. We drove there on a weekday morning (in my old un-air-conditioned pickup) as the temperature outside exceeded 100 degrees. By the time we arrived, we were tired and hot. I headed to the motel where I had previously stayed. We stopped on the way to grab some *slam food* (as my son calls it: food you don't have to fix. Just open and slam it) and went to the room to rest awhile until the heat of the afternoon cooled down.

I turned on the TV. We lay down on the bed to relax. We ate snacks and drank cold sodas. I had taken off my sweaty work pants and shirt to cool off. Shelly had taken off some of her clothes and put on one of my long tee shirts. As explained earlier, I hadn't set many boundaries. So that didn't seem unusual. We were watching a movie lying in a spooning position, me behind her. I had an arm around her when I dozed off for awhile. The next thing I knew I woke up to find that I had my hand down between her legs and was touching her clitoris. I had touched her, actually touched her!! My own daughter!! What was I doing? How could I have done that?

When I fully realized what had just happened a shiver of reality hit me like a bolt of lightning. I immediately got up and instructed her to put on her clothes. I put on mine, rushed straight outside and sat down on the tailgate of my truck in disbelief.

Thankfully I had not penetrated her. But how the hell could I have touched her? I was shocked! A sense of shame gripped me. I was utterly mortified. I remember her coming out to the back of the truck. I said, "Shelly. I'm your dad. I am sorry, so very sorry about what just happened." I was a wreck, disgusted and appalled at myself. I looked at her. I instantly knew that would be one of those things you can NEVER take back.

Memories of that little baby girl I brought home in that summer long ago suddenly came to mind which totally crushed what little self-respect I may have had left. Horror-struck, guilty and ashamed aren't enough to describe how I felt. I told her, "I don't know how but things are going to change.

Nothing like this will ever happen again." She looked at me and said," Don't worry, Dad. No big deal. Let's just forget about it." She acted like it didn't matter. I was torn and devastated. But just like I'd groomed her, she attempted to comfort **me** and implied **I** was off the hook. I knew better. Things were a mess. I had absolutely destroyed any trust or safety my daughter was entitled to feel around me. I was supposed to take care of her. I felt like a complete failure, appalled at what I had done. Tragically I had to "own" it completely.

I gathered myself up. It had cooled down some. I resumed work. Shelly helped. We somehow got done with the job without me sawing off my hand or hanging myself from one of the balconies before returning home.

We stayed a few days as was our previous plan and completed what I had gone there to do. Then we headed home. We discussed what had happened on the way home and agreed not to tell her mother. So in addition to molesting Shelly, I had coaxed her into conspiring with me to keep a *secret* from her mother, my wife.

Add another ingredient to the crazy soup mix.

That *incident* wasn't talked about for years after we got home. Nancy certainly wasn't told a thing. In order to better manage situations concerning my children I set badly needed and overdue boundaries. I took responsibility to behave differently in front of and around my kids. I knew I had to protect them from ME. I had to avoid placing them in vulnerable situations while I figured out what had made ME *cross the line*. **Unbelievable!** The guilt and ensuing shame I carried from my detestable act had grown into a tormenting inner voice judging everything I did. I completely "owned" the molest and felt as if a lurking demon had taken root within me bringing darkness and slowly draining my spirit. Then I suspected every move I made. I felt I had become an extremely inadequate father, just a counterfeit Dad. My dignity evaporated. My self-respect gone. Misery seemed all that remained.

9

Over the course of the next few years I continued to seek employment with the State while contracting construction jobs. One day in the fall of '89 I received a call from the California Highway Patrol inviting me to interview for a maintenance mechanic position. I still had my Contractor's license. But it was challenging to start a business with little money. So I took advantage of the opportunity and tried to appease Nancy. There were eighty-two applicants for one position. The field was narrowed to about five. Then the interviews were scheduled. I was the successful candidate and got the job. I finished any outstanding construction commitments and started to work for the Department in October.

My new job involved traveling throughout the state as part of a two man crew Tuesday morning through Friday evening. My partner and I built mountain-top radio sites and were responsible for back-up power generators at local Highway Patrol offices (911 centers). My confidence and self-esteem that had dwindled since I left the railroad began to grow.

My job skills earned me the respect of my fellow workers. I began to feel valued. Once again we had dependable income for our family. And when I got home on the weekends I had leftover "per diem" money too. Financially, times got much better. I worked only four days a week. So on most Mondays Nancy and the kids would go to work and school, respectively. I had a day to myself to do all the things it takes to run a family. I even managed to learn to play golf. My new job was a much appreciated blessing. It had variety, a casual pace, and *no stress*. Each project was unique and required traveling to a different location. I wasn't responsible for the cost of a project like I was as a self-employed contractor. I went home and didn't worry about money or the future. We had the next few years to climb out of debt and provide opportunities for our kids they had thus far been denied. Man! What a relief! I thought I had found my career job and settled in. We started dreaming of owning our own home again.

I remind you that our relationship 'cancer' was only in remission. What I had done to Shelly had planted a *bad* seed and was rotting. It was only a matter of time before "the fertilizer" hit me.

My being gone most of the time meant Nancy and I didn't have to continuously put up with each other. Our situation became tolerable.

Red Skelton used to say the secret to his marriage was, "My wife and I go out to dinner twice a week. I go on Mondays. She goes on Fridays." And "We sleep in separate beds. Hers is in California. Mine is in Texas."

But my absence also intensified the way the kids, all three then teenagers, and their mother treated each other. Everyone was driving everyone nuts. In addition to the usual parent/teenager stuff there was that "role shift." It was a powder keg ready to blow.

It's said time heals a lot of things. As time went on we were slowly embraced back into our "church family." The leadership had begun a program designed to promote adult couple friendships. It was called Food and Fellowship. If a couple was interested they signed up and were paired with two other couples. Once a month, over a three month period, each couple hosted the other two in their home for a social gathering. We enjoyed participating. After the three months were over, we'd switch and start again with new couples.

Shelly was just a few weeks short of her sixteenth birthday on a Friday night when one such social event was planned at another couples' home. When we arrived Nancy wasn't feeling good. So we stayed for only a short time and excused ourselves to return home so Nancy could go to bed and rest. When we arrived I opened the front door ahead of Nancy and went to the kitchen where Ann was baking cookies. She looked up at me with a "deer in the headlights" look on her face. Meanwhile, Nancy had followed me through the front door and headed upstairs to the bedrooms. All of a sudden I heard her scream, "What are you doing?" Shelly's room was right at the top of the stairs. She was on the bed in her room with her boyfriend. They were completely naked engaging in intercourse. I ran to see what was happening in time to hear Shelly respond in a smart-assed tone, "We're having sex Mom. What's it look like we're doing?" The boyfriend, scared to death, scrambled to gather his clothes trying to put his pants on while stumbling down the stairs and managed to get by me and out the door. He fumbled getting his shoes on, jumped on a bicycle and rode away as fast as he could. Nancy was ballistic. She stormed towards our room, grabbed the phone and called the police.

Soon our "church friend" and cop on patrol Les showed up. Nancy was infuriated. She adamantly wanted to press charges. Shelly's poor boyfriend was a week or so past his eighteenth birthday which made him an adult. A few minutes passed. The phone rang. It was the boyfriend calling to see if Shelly was "alright." Les took the phone, told him he was a police officer, asked where he was and if he could talk to him in person to get his side of the story. After he hung up the phone, he turned to us wanting to know what we thought should be done. Nancy was insistent that the kid should be charged with *raping* our daughter. Meanwhile a female officer arrived and took Shelly downstairs to separate her from us and find out what was really going on. Shelly's attitude was they were just teenagers having sex. What's the big deal?

Les got into his patrol car and left. He met the boyfriend down behind a local convenience store, busted him and took him to spend the weekend in the county jail before he could see the judge Monday morning. By then Nancy had cooled down a little. But there remained plenty of tension to go around. On Monday the boyfriend was arraigned on charges, given a court date and released. He was the only son of a single mother. They lived nearby. As his court date approached, I went to see the judge without Nancy's knowledge. I asked him to go easy on the kid. I wasn't happy with what had happened but I didn't think he had done something worthy of going to jail. And I was probably subconsciously feeling my own guilt. The judge asked me if the boy had a father. I said, "Yes. In Colorado, I think."

When the appointed court day arrived the judge invited the young man into his chambers. In so doing the judge dismissed the recorder and the actions in his chambers were "off the record." The judge offered him an opportunity to sign an *affidavit of guilt*.[9] He said that he would take the matter *under submission*[10] provided he left the State and did not return for a minimum of one year. If he agreed and complied, then after the year had passed the judge would drop the charges. It would all go away. No conviction. No record. That afternoon the boy got on the bus and left. Shelly told me some time later that she never saw him again but did talk to him on the phone a few years afterward.

---

[9] Affidavit of Guilt—signed in front of the judge and he took it, filed it privately for his own latter use.

[10] Under Submission—if the signer violated the agreement the judge could enter the affidavit in the record in lieu of a trial—guilty by agreement.

10

My Highway Patrol schedule was four days on during the week and three days off on weekends. While I was away Shelly acted out all sorts of behaviors (most of which I didn't have a clue about until she told me years later). "World War Three" was underway between her and her mother. Shelly was seeing a new boyfriend Kenny. As the "War" escalated in my absence she ran off with him causing all hell to break loose. Upon my return Nancy expected me to go get her because she knew exactly where they'd gone. She was staying with Kenny in a trailer on his grandparents rural property nearby. So I headed out alone and brought her back home. A few weeks later while I was gone working, "here we go again." That time I refused Nancy's demand to go get her. She became enraged. I said, "Let her go. When she tires of playing house she'll come home on her own." I was also afraid of blowing the cover off my own secret with Shelly. I went to work.

Several years every Tuesday morning I was up and off to work and returned home late Friday night. Nancy's and my relationship had stagnated to the point we were just going through the motions like some sort of wind-up dolls. On the mornings I left she would kiss me goodbye. I'd hug her and say, "I love you, see you Friday" and off I'd go relieved.

It was wintertime and dark by the time I had gotten home from work. On that particular Friday I returned to find all of the lights off when I drove into the driveway. Thinking that they must have gone somewhere earlier and forgot to turn on any welcoming lights I parked as usual and got out of my van, went to the door and opened it. The whole house was EMPTY! I was startled, shocked and immediately pissed off. There was just our little cocker spaniel staring at me with a look of despair on her face (matching mine, I'm sure). I investigated to find one twin-sized bed in our master bedroom and some of my clothes (that didn't fit Nancy) left in the closet. I was stunned. She must be spun! I had all the feelings from Tucson all over again. Where had she gone this time? WTF was she up to? AND WHERE WERE MY KIDS?

I found out later she had set in motion a plan to leave me weeks before and moved into a nearby apartment. When I left the previous Tuesday she made Mark and Ann stay home from school and "forced them" to help move. They didn't know what was going on. She wouldn't tell them. But it wasn't like they weren't familiar with her crazy shit. She went so far as to have Mark pack up all my tools and construction stuff. Then she moved it by herself to a rented storage facility without the kids knowing where it was. To add insult to injury she sold my truck which had a newly rebuilt engine, racks and a new tool box to a local police officer for a fraction of its value. When I figured that out I went to the police station to see the chief and told him what she had done, that I wanted my truck back. I asked if he would talk to the officer. He laughed at me. He said that if she signed the title legally, "too freaking" bad. I didn't know at the time he was sitting on a report and I was under investigation.

I didn't know what to make of her leaving. Shit. I figured that the "bipolar express" had just made another roller-coaster loop around the track. I had a three day weekend to make some sense of all of it. I found the kids and where she'd gone (with a little help from my next door neighbor, John). I talked to Nancy and agreed we needed some time away from each other. No kidding! Tuesday came. I went back to work.

I was working on a project on the eastern side of the Sierra Nevada Mountains in a remote area a couple of hundred miles away. Wednesday afternoon I got a call from the local area commander of the Highway Patrol requesting me to come down to the office. We interrupted what we were doing, packed up our tools and returned to the office to see what was up. My work partner, Dave and I had spent the previous evening at the commanders' home and had dinner with his family. He was a great guy. When we entered his office he got up with a very somber look on his face; he told Dave to wait down the hall and shut the door. He told me to take a seat. As I sat he looked around at me with a blank look on his face, took a deep breath and said he had just gotten a call from Sacramento headquarters. He was told they had an indictment for my arrest. They had instructed him to arrest me, place me in custody and make arrangements to transfer me back to Sacramento. He seemed sad and reluctant as he cuffed me. I thought it was some sick joke since I'd participated in other shenanigans before and in a few minutes the whole office would come in with Dave and have a good laugh at my expense, take those damn bracelets off and then get down to business. Never having been cuffed before I was feeling somewhat nervous. I wondered maybe this wasn't a joke. Oh shit! Why did they bust me? I hadn't done anything. The commander left his office and went down the hall leaving me alone to think about things. I hadn't seen or heard from Dave. Then it dawned on me that they might have him "locked-down" in another room since they wouldn't tell me "why" I was arrested. Thinking since Dave had been with the department for many years prior to me and was not bashful about "helping himself" to State owned equipment we were both on the hot seat for something he had done. His being a former Navy guy with honor and glory and all that stuff I thought he would man-up and confess, take responsibility for his sticky fingers and they'd let me go.

The commander returned. After a long period of silence and a few more calls for clarification he informed me I was being charged with *molesting* my daughter. Those terrible words, *molesting my daughter* again began ringing in my head. It had been three or four years since I had touched her. I had tried to distance myself from that dark day. There had been *absolutely no inappropriate behavior* since. I immediately felt the weight of shame lurking from that dark demon as it raised its ugly inner accusing voice. I became discouraged. I felt hopeless. What to do now? Things looked pretty bleak.

The Department had a logistics problem arresting me as I was the only qualified commercial driver licensed to operate their boom truck which I had driven to the work site. The commander didn't want that big truck left at his office and he didn't want to have one of his officers drive me in a patrol car two hundred miles to Sacramento. So he called headquarters. He convinced them that I could drive their truck back to Sacramento, stopping at three different offices on the way so they could keep tabs on me until I got back to the shop in Sacramento. They reached agreement. He took off the cuffs and bid me farewell. When I arrived at my destination it was after hours. So the department decided to allow me to leave the truck, get my personal van and "released" me with the promise of taking myself to County jail the following Monday for processing. Thinking I would be able to post bail and return to work the next Tuesday morning I left.

Before Nancy and the kids moved to the apartment, Shelly had grown tired of being away from home. "Playing house" with Kenny wasn't all she thought it would be. She wanted to come home but was scared of being grounded or her Mom and me taking some other disciplinary measures. So Kenny suggested that they go to the local police and tell them that she had run away because her dad was "messing" with her. They figured if they told the police I had "messed" with her it would get her off the hook for having run away. So that's what they did.

The police (and later the school counselors) were, of course, sympathetic to Shelly and used her reports to investigate me. They gave all they had to the District Attorney's office. The DA, in turn, contacted the Internal Affairs Branch of the Highway Patrol.

11

Shelly had many unfair burdens placed on her during those adolescent years. In addition to my despicable behavior her mother had relinquished her maternal responsibility and left Shelly to struggle under such an unnaturally heavy load. As I mentioned earlier, her mother was "absent" while in the present and constantly consumed by her own past. It wasn't her fault but the opportunity to do something about it and heal the pain was available too many times for no measurable change to have happened. As a result, Mark and Ann came to rely on Shelly not their mother for basic care. Shelly resented that. And Nancy had also shared way too much detail about her own childhood trauma with Shelly treating her as if she was a grown girlfriend instead of our teenaged daughter. It was no surprise the reported allegations of my molesting Shelly had paralleled many of the specific things which happened to her mother. At first the authorities were trying to assess the impact of the allegations on Shelly. Nancy was furious at me. I was the MONSTER. She seemed more focused on seeing that I paid then treating our daughter. Her older brother (remember? the police officer) never was held accountable for all he'd done to her. There'd been no justice then and, by God, there was going to be this time! She was **relentless.**

There was a time for blame, of course, a time for counseling, a reasonable price to pay and a then a time to heal and move forward. But Nancy would have none of it. She went ballistic. Then have a change of heart (or a bipolar flip-flop), calm down and insist all she wanted was for us to "get help" to come to terms with what had happened to Shelly. She even offered to keep it only between us and the counselors. Then KABOOM! She couldn't stand it. She called the cops and made a giant case out of it. But once the cops were in it she couldn't backtrack and have it both ways, especially since I worked for a law enforcement agency.

About a month before I was formally charged, I was ordered to report downtown to the Internal Affairs Department of the Highway Patrol for an interview. IA is extremely skilled at getting to the bottom of just about anything. Two officers brought me into a small room and started to interrogate me. I was unfamiliar with interrogation so I asked them if I needed representation. They said I didn't. They were very forceful and since I was a state worker I was compelled to cooperate and answer their questions. I wanted to know if I was the subject of their investigation. They ignored my inquiry. I was interrogated in excess of eight hours with no more than a bathroom break. No union representation. No lawyer. They insisted that I didn't need either unless I thought I did because I had done something that might require one. The whole line of vigorous questioning was about how I grew up, my extended family, my church connections, my co-workers and my job. There was never a hint that they were coming after me on a molest allegation. When they approached the subject of my marriage I informed them that we were in counseling for certain things. I did not elaborate. When they tried to turn up the heat I told them I was taking advantage of my employee benefits. Nancy and I were working with a counselor on issues concerning our marriage and dealing with Shelly. All counseling prior to the allegations was initiated by me trying to do what I thought best for our family situation. I was trying to move forward. The molest issue had **not** become part of the counseling. I knew that if it was disclosed to Nancy everything would become all about her and nothing productive would be done. It had taken a back seat to other issues between Shelly and her mother and the family dynamic. (I was unaware at the time that the molestation could have been motivation for Shelly acting out.) After the interrogation concluded I still hadn't a clue where they were going or who they were after.

IA had investigated every report given them by the DA, interviewed everyone who may have had any knowledge about me and did so without me suspecting that **I** was their target. They spent a significant number of hours and resources investigating my whole life. They presented their findings to the local county DA's office in a brief as thick as a phone book. That report was the basis of the complaint filed against me. The term "molest" seemed rather vague and general. I wasn't informed of the actual charges until I was in custody. And that wasn't until I returned with their boom truck and took myself to the County Jail. I wondered how they allowed me to run around out of custody for days before I reported to jail and post a relatively small bail if I was such a pervert and danger to society and my family according to the charges. They must have known more than they let on or they were being pushed.

I was devastated when I first read the **actual** charges. I was charged in California with one count of violating the

State Penal Code section 288.5[11] which "**requires** that there is **continuous sexual abuse** with a minor under the age of fourteen involving **substantial sexual contact** at least **three or more times** in excess of more than a three month period **involving penetration of the vagina or rectum with a penis or foreign object, oral copulation, and/or masturbation.**" I WAS FURIOUS! Certainly what I was guilty of was serious and inappropriate contact. But NEVER was there any penetration OF anything WITH anything! All the reported allegations seemed patterned after some of the acts committed on Nancy. Not anything close to what I actually did.

Let me make things perfectly clear from my point of view. I am now only addressing the charges from a legal standpoint. I was charged with a much more severe crime than the **facts** supported. I was **not** guilty of *sustained sexual contact* as defined by the law. I **never** penetrated. Period. End of story. I was **never** aroused nor did I fantasize anything of a sexual nature. I did NOT get any sexual gratification at the expense of my daughter. I'm not discounting the serious emotional

---

[11] Penal Code 288.5, defined: law.onecle.com/california/penal/288.5.html

impact on Shelly but the **facts** were supposed to determine the charge.

I liken it to a person charged with first degree murder when the *facts* supported involuntary manslaughter. From a legal point of view a very big difference. But from a practical point of view, in either case, there is still a dead body. And a dead body is a dead body! And a molest is still a molest as far as Shelly and I were concerned. I am guilty of a "dead body" so to speak. I cannot deny I molested my daughter. I want to **stress** I know any act I was guilty of was damaging to Shelly. She was my daughter, a minor in my care and tragically became my victim.

What I take issue with is since the local DA's office involved the larger State Department of the Highway Patrol, which is a paramilitary organization, there was no way for them to back off on the severity of the legal charges when later it became time to settle the case (plea bargain contract). The Highway Patrol had no axe to grind with me. In fact they loved my performance and valued me as an employee.

The State and the court system have a variety of remedies to dispense *appropriate* punishment for virtually every sex related crime possible. The degree to which I was prosecuted by the DA far exceeded what I had done. But the small county DA's office had passed the case to the Patrol. When the Patrol finished they gave the results back to the DA. Normally the DA's office would have investigated a complaint with their own resources and determined the *appropriate* charge(s). But since I was an employee of a law enforcement agency, they capitalized on having my *employer* do their work for them. Do you think any other employer would do that? After seeking such a request, the DA's office couldn't back off and ever expect such a level of cooperation in the future.

I was determined to fight the charges. I hired an attorney, posted bail and resumed my duties at work pending upcoming court dates. I was restricted to no travel and wasn't assigned any duties (other than to show up and literally sit in the shop and communicate with no one for almost six months I read a lot. So much for "presumption of innocence."

Pending the charges and until things were settled in court, I had no place to live. All of my resources went toward my legal fees to fight to stay out of prison. I lived in an old van I'd had for camping and learned to become an "urban" camper. That's a whole other book. But I will say even though I was living in a van I managed to keep myself clean and kept up my appearance. Did you know you can walk onto any community college campus, go to the sports complex and shower and shave without anyone questioning your being there? That's because everyone on a college campus is considered an adult and no children are around (with the apparent exception of Penn State??). As long as I had a clean appearance and nice shirt I could go to any large funeral or wedding and most likely end up with something to eat. So being hungry or being dirty was no excuse (just a tip about homeless "urban" camping).

The legal process was somewhat slow and took its own toll. I was focused on fighting the specifics of the facts until it became painfully clear what I was up against. In our society, even though we're taught there is a presumption of innocence, when one is charged with a sex crime, especially if a minor is involved, one is guilty until *proven innocent*. And folks, that just ain't going to happen.

As the day of my pre-trial hearing approached things began to take shape. In our system nobody wants to go to trial. It's costly and takes a lot of time. The only ones who do are the defendants who can afford the big dollar defense teams to crush the usually new "right out of law school" assistant DA's prosecuting attorneys. It became "Let's Make a Deal" time. I was preparing to fight the fight of my life. My attorney had other plans. After discussing the case with the prosecutor he sat me down and told me the offer. I argued if the severity of the charge was changed, I would have no problem pleading guilty. I wasn't trying to get them to lessen the charge to avoid prison rather just to make it appropriate to the facts. Then I'd deal with the outcome. I was concerned I was being prosecuted as a ***preferential predator***[12] of children instead of a ***situational offender*** limited to a family member under specific circumstances. On my own I had already successfully instituted new boundaries around my kids to avoid repeating any situations likely to endanger them.

My attorney tried desperately to get the prosecutor to change the charges to fit the *actual* crime. But it became clear it was a *political issue* between the DA's office and the Highway Patrol. If the DA lessened the charge after all the energy the Patrol invested his office would forever be met with reluctance should it request cooperation again. That just wasn't going to happen. I also suspected Nancy had played a

---

[12] wikipedia.org/wiki/Situational_offender

part in determining the prosecutors' hard-line position. But I was never able to confirm it.

Referring to my previous analogy the DA was going to make me plead guilty to *first degree murder* but sentence me for *involuntary manslaughter.* If I pled guilty (the plea bargain contract) the following conditions would apply:

1. I would be allowed to resign from the Highway Patrol instead of being fired as a result of a felony conviction. That would preserve my right to re-hire with the State in my classification after my probation period was completed.
2. I would be given a State prison term of 16 years which the judge would suspend keeping me out of prison as long as I didn't violate probation.
3. I would be admitted to formal probation (a privilege) for 5 years and serve 8 months in the local County jail.
4. I would enroll in and complete a court recognized counseling program.
5. I would pay restitution and court cost
6. I would be required to **register as a sex offender**.

7. I would give up *some* of my civil rights.

8. I would be given a promise to have the conviction expunged (removed from the record) if and after I successfully completed my probation.

They gave me about an hour to process my choices.

Now some of you think you would fight to the death to not have a conviction like that on your record. I completely understand. Some of you may be thinking I should be put away for good or even "thrown into the shredder." I understand that too. Others may be thinking the offer was too light. I can understand that as well.

I'll discuss further what that offer really meant. But I will tell you for the first time in my life I actually relied on the opinions of others including my attorney. I even went to the "trunk" and sought God's counsel. I was facing 16 years in State prison if I refused the offer, was tried and convicted even if I was found guilty of a lesser, more appropriate crime.

My attorney sat me down and described the trial process (if I elected to go forward with my fight). First, the trial would begin with the police officer and/or the school counselors taking the stand. I would be in front of a "stacked" jury because the prosecution would make sure they all had children. They most likely would be State workers in the local area (since they seem to be about the only ones who can't get out of jury duty). Next, the reports would be read and entered into the record. Following that maybe Shelly would even take the stand and tell her side of things which could be less than the charges. I thought, "Great! I would be acquitted. Right?" Even if Shelly recanted everything the prosecutor would march an *expert* up to educate the jury on **child accommodation syndrome**[13] when the victim is the child of the accused and doesn't want her father to go to prison. In any case, you're going to be found guilty and go to prison for a very long time. Period. Take the deal. The clock is ticking. I took the deal.

Once I made the decision to accept the offer from the DA, I had to appear in open court in front of the judge. None of the particulars of the "deal" were put into the record. All they wanted to hear was "guilty." The judge pulled out his "boiler plate" cue card and asked me a series of questions. The following is the actual court minutes:

---

[13] Child Accommodation Syndrome–Retraction—www.secasa.com.au/index. php/workers/25/31

XXXXXXXXXX, California

September 28,1992

—oOo—

The matter of the People of the State of California, Plaintiff, versus R LUTHER COOPER,[14] Defendant, Case Number SCR-XXXX, came on regularly this day before the Honorable J. Richard Colls, Judge of the Superior Court of the State of California, County of XXXXX, Department Number Seven thereof.

The People were represented by MARK FRANCIS, Deputy District Attorney in and for the County of XXXXX, State of California.

Defendant was in personal attendance upon the Court, and he was represented by KATHLEEN BENTON, Deputy Public Defender in and for the County of XXXXX, State of California, acting as his counsel.

The following proceedings were had, to wit:

—oOo—

---

[14] All names changed from actual Court transcript

THE COURT: The next matter is People versus Cooper, case number XXX.

The defendant is present in Court with Counsel, Miss Benton, and District Attorney, Mr. Francis.

The matter is for—

MS. BENTON; Your Honor, it's Mr. Cooper's intention today to enter a plea of guilty to violation of Penal Code Section 288.5 with an indication, I believe, that the Court had made of eight to twelve months, assuming there's a favorable 288.1[15] report.

THE COURT: That's correct.

Mr. Cooper, did you understand the circumstances that's indicated by counsel?

THE DEFENDANT: Yes, I do, your Honor.

THE COURT: All right.

And I'm going to ask you the questions which I've just asked the previous Defendant, which relates your rights and the consequences of your plea.

So please, listen carefully.

And if you do not understand something, please ask Miss Benton to explain it to you.

---

[15]Probation report

First of all, with respect to the charges pending against you; do you understand that you have the right to a speedy and public trial by a jury?

You have the right to assistance of an attorney at all stages of proceedings.

And you have the right to be confronted by the witnesses against you.

And you have the power of the Court to order into Court any witnesses, who you may want to testify on your behalf.

And you have the right to present evidence on your behalf in defense of the charges.

And you have the privilege against self-incrimination.

Do you understand that you have all of these rights?

THE DEFENDANT: Yes, I do.

THE COURT: Do you understand that if you plead guilty, you're giving up all those rights, except the right to a lawyer?

THE DEFENDANT: Yes, I do, your Honor.

THE COURT: Do you know what a jury trial is?

THE DEFENDANT: Yes, I do.

THE COURT: Could you please tell me in your own words what you think it is?

THE DEFENDANT: It's a trial in front of 12 jurors, who determine, based on the tier of fact, the guilt or innocence.

THE COURT: You understand that if you plead guilty, you are giving up that right?

THE DEFENDANT: Yes, I do.

THE COURT: Do you give it up?

THE DEFENDANT: I do.

THE COURT: Counsel join in the waiver?

MS. BENTON: Yes, your Honor.

THE COURT: You also understand, since you're not going to trial, you're also giving up your right to confrontation of witnesses? That is, you're giving up your right to see, hear, and have your attorney question all witnesses, who might have been called to testify?

THE DEFENDANT: Yes, I do.

THE COURT: You also understand that by pleading guilty, you're giving up your right to remain silent, and to require the District Attorney to prove the case against you?

THE DEFEDANT: Yes, I understand that.

THE COURT: Please tell me in your own words, what you're pleading guilty to.

THE DEFENDAT: I'm pleading guilty to Penal Code Section 288.5. I read it, and I understand it.

THE COURT: And did you discuss with your attorney what the District Attorney would have been required to prove, in order for the jury to find you guilty of that offense?

THE DEFENDANT: Yes, I have.

THE COURT: Do you understand that crime is a felony?

THE DEFENDAT: Yes, I do your Honor.

THE COURT: Now, you are eligible for probation, and it can be for up to five years.

And I can require that you serve up to one year in the County Jail.

And I can impose a fine and restitution fine of up to $10,000 each.

And I can impose other conditions, which might relate to you or your offense.

Do you understand that?

THE DEFENDANT: I do.

THE COURT: Now, in the event that probation is denied or in the event that you violate your terms of probation and are sentenced to state prison, at that time the sentence may be 72 months, 144 months or 192 months, as the Court will determine.

Do you understand that?

THE DEFENDANT: Yes, sir.

THE COURT: You also understand that you can be required to serve a period of parole for up to five years following your release from prison, And if you did go to state prison, and you later commit a crime for which you're again sent to state prison; depending on the nature of this offense, and the later offense, your second sentence may be increased by up to five years, simply because you've served the prior prison term.

And finally, there's a $100 and up to a $10,000 fine imposed on every state prison commitment.

You understand that?

THE DEFENDANT: Yes, I do.

THE COURT: Are you now on probation or parole out of any Court for any reason, whatsoever?

THE DEFENDANT: No, I am not.

THE COURT: Are you a citizen of this country, having been born here?

THE DEFENDANT: Yes, I am.

THE COURT: Have you talked about this case with youe attorney?

THE DEFENDANT: Yes, I have.

THE COURT: Have you told her all the facts and circumstances that are known to you about the case?

THE DEFENDANT: Yes, sir.

THE COURT: Have you had enough time to talk to her?

THE DEFENDANT: Yes, sir.

THE COURT: Are you pleading guilty, because, in truth and in fact, you are guilty?

THE DEFENDANT: Yes, sir.

THE COURT: Other than as stated at the beginning of this hearing, have there been any promises made to you, in order to get you to plead guilty?

THE DEFENDANT: No, sir.

THE COURT: Have you pleading guilty, freely and voluntarily?

THE DEFENDANT: Yes, I am.

THE COURT: Do you understand that I will require that you waive your right to appeal as a condition of this plea?

THE DEFENDANT: Yes, sir.

THE COURT: Miss Benton, have you had enough time to discuss this case with your client?

MS. BENTON: I have, and also Mr. Schultz from my office.

THE COURT: Thank you.

And has your office discussed with him, his rights, defenses, and the possible consequences of the plea?

MS. BENTON: Yes, your Honor.

THE COURT: Do you join in the waiver of the other rights made by your client?

MS. BENTON: Yes, I join.

THE COURT: You stipulate there's a factual basis for the plea?

And you stipulate that the transcript of the Preliminary Examination or police reports prepared in this case may be used for that purpose?

MS. BENTON: Yes, your Honor.

THE COURT: All right.

Mr. Cooper, then to Count One, charging a violation of Penal Code Section 288.5, sexual abuse of a child, a felony, occurring on or about November 1st, 1986 to June 30, 1989; how do you plead?

THE DEFENDANT: Guilty, your Honor.

THE COURT: Do you waive your right to appeal?

THE DEFENDANT: I do.

THE COURT: I accept the plea.

I find the Defendant understands his Constitutional Rights, the nature of the charges against him, and the consequences of the plea.

I find that the Defendant has voluntarily and knowingly waived his Constitutional Rights.

I find that there's a factual basis for the entry of plea, and that it has been voluntarily entered.

Trial dates and other appearances are vacated.

Waive time?

MS. BENTON: Yes, we'll waive time for sentencing.

Your Honor, he's also attempting to seek other employment.

As a result of this plea, he's going to be losing his job. And we would like to have a little extra time on the sentencing in this case.

THE COURT: Well, I'll set it for December 7th, which is really quite a ways down the road. December 7th at 8:30.

Dr. Johns will be appointed to conduct an evaluation under Penal Code Section 288.1 in connection with the probation report.

The Defendant is ordered to return on the date set with counsel.

Thank you.

MS. BENTON: Thank you, your Honor.

MR. FRANCIS: Thank you, your Honor.

(Proceedings concluded.)

So you see I plead guilty and put myself completely at the court's mercy. That's the process. The judge accepted my guilty plea and set a date to sentence me. Next case.

Regardless of any "deal" the law required that after a guilty plea was entered I had to be evaluated to determine if I was "suitable" for probation. In California probation is a **privilege** that may or may not include jail time. I was ordered to go to a court-appointed psychiatrist for testing.

The entire process from the day I was informed of my indictment until I pled guilty was approximately seven months.

12

It was a long, hot, dry Central Valley California summer and while the criminal charge was awaiting the upcoming court dates I was under a restraining order barring me from seeing or even talking to my kids. Since I had been charged with a "sex crime" I was immediately ripped away from any contact with my family until it was settled. I spent most of my time isolated at work reading or away from work tormented by the uncertainty of my future and feeling very lonely. After a few months of soul searching and contemplating what was ahead, I decided to "clean up" some of the mistakes I'd made in the past. I thought if I should lose my battle to stay free, perhaps I should take the time I had before the conclusion of my prosecution to attend to things that had been on my mind.

One of my deepest regrets (and dumbest mistakes) was to burden Alyssa with the mess I'd made in Tucson during my *first divorce* (the one I withdrew). As much as I truly loved the time we were together, the circumstances couldn't have been worse. Obviously I needed time to adapt to the changes I was going to have to make without having turned our friendship into a relationship. I should have focused on my children especially at the ages they were then. The despair I felt from not being in contact with my kids undermined any ability to resist the persuasion of my former pastor and his buddies. Six years had elapsed since leaving Alyssa and her son Adam. I hadn't seen or heard from her during that time. I set out to see if I could find her and, at the very least, own up to the damage and suffering I'd caused them. Through my Highway Patrol contacts, I was able to access the computer system to locate her. I was aware of the possibility (or probability) she may not want to have anything to do with me. I found out she was living on the peninsula in the San Francisco Bay area and working in medicine. It was about a two hour drive from where I was "doing time" at the Highway Patrol facilities. I decided to drive after work the next Friday to the area where she lived. I was "camping" anyway. I spent the night near her home in my van.

Being a Christian I believed that God does his best work in our lives when we slow down enough to consider His direction, give Him the opportunity to unfold our paths as we go. It's amazing how that happens! A little faith yields a whole lot of blessings. Nothing is by accident. Nothing is by luck. Looking back on what was about to happen I can see His hand clearly in the timing and circumstances. I had been *moved* to contact Alyssa. Little did I know how significant that would be.

Just the day before Alyssa had received sad news about medical testing she had been undergoing to determine the cause of symptoms she had been experiencing. Her doctor's diagnosis was Multiple Sclerosis (MS). She had worked so hard to establish a career, had struggled to raise a son alone and was optimistic about her future. Since I left her in Southern California she had not even allowed herself to be in a relationship. She was focused instead on her job and her son. Then **MS** happened.

With what was determined to be the progressive form of the disease she knew it would be only a matter of time until she wouldn't be able to work anymore. Adam was almost eighteen and would want to be out on his own soon. Alyssa lay in bed that night sad, crying, feeling lonely and depressed. She thought to herself, "who would want me now?" She was heartbroken.

The next morning, can you believe it? The very next morning! I called her. I had to muster the courage and accept that she could just hang up because of my cowardly departure years earlier. I even thought, "what if a man answers? What if Adam does?" When she answered the phone she could hardly believe it was me. I asked if I could come over. She requested a few hours to ready herself, straighten up the house and then certainly I could. When I knocked on the door she came, opened it and we hugged each other for a long time. I knew then our friendship would somehow survive the past.

There was nothing defective in Alyssa. She most certainly was the same spirit I first met way back in the eighth grade. We connected as 'long lost friends.' We agreed not to jump into anything, to take it slowly and reconnect our friendship. Besides I hadn't told her about the molestation yet. That would come soon but for the time being we just wanted to enjoy each other's company. Slowly over the next weeks or months, I disclosed everything to her. I told her what I had done during one of our long phone calls while I was away "working" and she was thoroughly shocked. She asked to be alone for awhile to think about what I'd just said. She was carrying the unknown affects of her newly discovered disease and trying to determine whether or not to have me with all my "baggage" become a part of her life again. I understood and gave her all the time she needed.

Alyssa has a lot of faith in God. She prayed seeking some direction and comfort. After some time she came to the conclusion she loved me. No matter what happened, she still loved me. She had the ability and history to see me for who I was and not for what I had or hadn't done. She struggled not to judge me. But she was able to separate me as a person from the events I was responsible for causing. It wasn't easy. But she decided to stand by me as I faced a daunting ordeal. She reserved commitment towards any relationship beyond our friendship. Her plate was already pretty much full.

I started spending my weekends in the Bay area with Alyssa and my boring work week in Sacramento waiting for the disposition of my case. Alyssa was encouraging and supportive. She alone stood beside me, an *accused sex offender.* And I was there for her as she confronted the MS, struggling to understand the disease and the direction her life was going to take. We grew together mutually supporting each other.

I'll jump forward to tell you we spent the summer and into the fall getting back together. She inspired me to become a better person and to make better choices in my life. The decision to reconnect our friendship was one of the smartest moves I've ever made. I think I can say hers as well. We are still together today. She is my "beautiful queen." I see no disease, no defect, only the bright soul and energetic spirit she has always been. Alyssa is my love. She makes me laugh and enjoy life. I would like to think I'm still her "prince" after all these years, even her "magnificent king," though I might be trapped in an overweight, middle-aged body with a bumper sticker. CAUTION: REGISTRERED CITIZEN. But we get by that.

13

Taking the deal opened a new chapter in my life. I resigned from the Patrol and made arrangements to be evaluated by the court-appointed psychiatrist. My initial visit to his office was to be interviewed and tested to determine if I was *suitable* for probation. If he concluded I was not I would be sent to State Prison for what could be up to *eighteen years!* Needless to say, that visit was extremely important. It would dramatically impact the direction my life would take. I was so anxious (bordering on panic) I made sure I was at his office about a half hour before my scheduled time. I used that time to try to calm myself down and relax. THIS WAS SERIOUS. It wasn't like taking a school test or even having a job interview. It was opening up to someone I'd never met before and letting him roam around in my head not knowing what he may come up with. I had nothing to hide. But I wasn't exactly confident in myself either.

While waiting I received a "page" (no cell phones then) from my children's mother. Nancy had known the exact time of my appointment. I don't know how she knew. But she did. Based on our agreement at the time, I was to return her pages if she had something to discuss regarding our kids. I asked to use the office phone. When she answered my call she yelled at me, "Shelly is pregnant! Have a nice day asshole!" Then she slammed the phone down hanging up on me.

"Excuse me sir. The doctor will see you now."

Fortunately, he was there to clinically evaluate me and not morally judge me. He was great. I told him what had just happened. He said to relax. We'd talk about it as well as any other things that were pertinent. After a number of return visits to his office during the next few weeks and completing a battery of psychological testing[16], I was found **suitable** for probation. **Relieved**!-Wow, I wasn't going to prison. I was facing sixteen years in the pen and suddenly only probation for five years; no comparison. You can imagine I was extremely grateful just at the chance to do whatever was needed to recover my life. Afterword the doctor's evaluation report was prepared for the

---

[16] Dr. Johns used the MMPI, Minnesota Multiphasic Personality Inventory, Clinical Assessment wikipedia.org/wiki/Minnesota_Multiphasic_Personality _Inventory

probation department and the court. He provided me a copy but I have since misplaced it. I'd prefer to share his findings by quoting him directly. But the best I can do is to hit on the main points I remember. First he found that my prior living conditions, particularly my relationship with Nancy, were key contributors to my offense. He wasn't excusing my behavior or blaming Nancy, just an objective observation that contributed to what I did. He noted that condition had been remedied by divorce. Then more importantly he determined I was a *situational sex offender.* My offense was associated with my situation and was unlikely to be repeated. He found I was **not** considered a *preferential offender,* an offender having a preferential or *predatory* behavior (I didn't stalk kids). He determined I did **not** have *any pedophilic tendencies* and was **not** violent. My previous behavior had been limited to my family and specifically my oldest daughter. He concluded since the circumstances had changed the probability I would re-offend was very slight to non-existent. Therefore, in his professional opinion I was **suitable** for probation posing no threat to the public.

I returned to court to receive my sentence in mid-December shortly after Thanksgiving. The judge pretty much followed the previously agreed to *plea deal* which suspended any state prison time but included a county jail sentence. I was allowed to leave and given a date to report. The judge was generous in giving me about four weeks to put my affairs in order. That allowed me to remain free through the holidays before I was to start my jail time in early January.

Alyssa and I were happy and thankful to spend the holidays together. We had discussed her relocating away from the Bay Area as her MS was making it more difficult to continue working and she needed to find a less expensive area in which to live. We wanted to get her moved and settled before I had to go serve time. The terms of my formal probation required me to secure advance approval from the probation department as to where I could live after completing jail. So we chose a suitable location in the northern part of Sacramento County near the XXXXX County line as I had been prosecuted in XXXXX County. Sacramento County offered to supervise my probation as a courtesy to XXXXX County allowing us to locate close to Alyssa's medical need providers. This was critical to meeting her needs and workable for me later.

Although sentenced to eight months I only served three weeks "inside." Due to continuous over-crowded conditions at the main jail and since it was my first conviction I was going to be allowed "out" of jail conditioned upon wearing an electronic GPS monitoring device on my ankle provided we could pay the associated cost. Alyssa then disabled sacrificed and paid for the monitor. I never liked how strict probation was and I don't envy the officers that deal with it. But in my case, though, the Sacramento guys always treated me well. They were respectful as long as I followed the rules. That was my challenge. Growing up I was use to getting by and bending the rules "just a little." Remember?

Once out of jail, XXXXX County probation allowed me to work as long as they determined the job was appropriate. The only approved work I got with an ankle bracelet was a minimum wage job in a plant nursery about 40 minutes from where I lived but in close proximity to the jail. Probation required constant supervision and extremely limited contact with the public. I found out later the owner of the nursery was one of the "good ol' boys" with the people running the jail supplying him with a steady, reliable, low-wage work force. In retrospect the job was unofficially "arranged" by the probation department and I was encouraged to go "there" to find work. So this initial phase of my "privileged" probation amounted to a nothing short of a modern-day forced labor camp with benefits. I was relieving the over-crowded situation at the main jail, barely earning enough to offset what we were contributing towards the county's monitoring scam program and my gas expenses to remain "free." The alternative was to return to jail to a solitary "protective" cell.

I spent the spring and summer working in a dirt-shed at that nursery. The dirt-shed was the place where all the planting soil was mixed, sterilized and placed in pots or on racks before anything was planted in it. I could leave home at a specific time, go straight to work, and return by a certain time or be in **violation** of my release terms which could result in a new separate felony charge. All my movements were monitored continuously by the "bracelet" on my ankle.

Alyssa's MS limited her ability to walk and she had not yet been able to acquire an electric scooter. Since she was unable to go out on her own I was allowed one hour on Sunday mornings for grocery shopping. Once I left a full cart of groceries in line at the store racing home to be there before my time expired. Just to get the basic needs put a real strain on both of us. She "shared" my probation by not being physically able to leave the house the entire time I was on the monitor. She also surrendered her privacy by agreeing to allow the officers to search our home anytime. We were not allowed any fire arms or alcohol whatsoever. They showed up unannounced any hour of the day, night and weekends for surprise inspections.

Next time you buy plants think about the dirt they're planted in. It has to be mixed and cooked in a hot oven to kill germs and weeds before planting whatever you're buying. Working in the dirt shed was a hot, nasty job. I had to bring my own lunch and remain in that manure-shit-stinking filthy barn all day and at noon-time eat if the flies didn't eat it first. Only good thing about it was it wasn't jail. But there were a few days a XXXXX probation officer came by the job and just to screw with me he'd cuff and chain me inside the shed to remind me I was still in custody, returning at the end of work to let me go home. That made the corner of the shed the restroom, the length of the chain. I could take a leak on the manure pile or add too it if I had too.

Probation was an **extremely** humbling experience. I lost **all** my rights and was treated like a child by not being allowed to make any decisions. In jail I had to ask for everything, even permission to go to the toilet and take a shower. Additional privileges had to be earned. But I adapted to my circumstances and was conditionally released to finish the rest of my sentence at home under the "house arrest."

There is however another kind of "jail" when convicted as a *sex offender*. It is a *mental* jail. Shame and its crippling effects brought lots of despair, depression and dejection. There were times I lost complete hope in the future. I had no idea what work I could get after getting "off" the monitor. Most of that time back then is a blur to me now. Fortunately I don't recall many of the details while on that damn "bracelet." I know I went to work daily at the dirt-shed and returned straight home each night stopping only for gas. Money was tight and Alyssa's MS was getting worse. As time wore on, I became overwhelmed by the stress of being treated like a slave at work and adapting to this new scourge of being a convicted *sex offender*. Sometimes I would become despondent, breakdown and just cry. It seemed I had lost so much. I experienced times when I couldn't remember the day's events. Alyssa recalls times when I just checked out mentally. She had to hold and comfort me like a little child. I was continuously haunted by nightmares and emotionally drained. The shame and stigma were gripping. It wasn't good for Alyssa's MS which is greatly affected by stress. My crap was a truckload for her to take on and eventually, me and all my stuff became too much of a burden on her. When I finished the custody time and got that leash off my leg, she had no alternative but to ask me to leave for her own good. It was really bringing down her ability to take care of herself with me around. I packed the few things I had into my van. We broke up again but this time I had not abandoned her so much as I honored her and respected her circumstances enough to free her from all my burdens. I was lost, scared and broke with nowhere to live. But I wasn't under any circumstances going back to that miserable dirt-shed for a meager minimum paycheck. I was headed to a real crossroads in my life. Some say you have to "hit bottom" in order to turn your life around. I felt like I was looking **up** to the bottom.

14

After I completed my months in custody I was released back to freedom with supervision. Probation required that I had to have a place to live (so the officers could check up on me). Problem was I was out of work. I had nowhere to live and a poor credit history. Renting a place was out of the picture. I was nearing a deadline or face being *in violation* and have to go back to court and possibly **prison**. It was a high stress time. But I was determined not to give up. My earlier jail confinement and my dirt-shed experience was enough to motivate me to keep searching for a solution. Besides I owed it to myself and my kids to do something I could be proud of.

I was pretty messed up emotionally. I avoided thinking about my 'issues' and instead spent most of my effort trying to find somewhere to live and start my life over. It was a day to day deal. I didn't have very much confidence left and was starting to become scared. Used to be as long as there was opportunity out there I could take advantage of it (even if it meant bending the rules *just a little*). Suddenly things were different. I was a *sex offender* and a *convicted felon on formal probation.*

I continued my search. Within a few weeks I met Ted a middle-aged man who had just lost his elderly father. He and his wife needed some work done on his father's home to ready it for tenants. Behind his father's house was an attached makeshift room with its own small bathroom and a phone. Ted let me move into it if I promised to be a caretaker and agreed to do the work needed. I was *extremely* grateful. I can't describe the feeling I had that someone would take a chance on me. I was required to disclose to him what I had done and gain probation's approval to live there. *But I had an address and a phone*! If you have never been homeless you probably can't relate to how depressing and frustrating it can be. It's not just being without a place to live. You have to have the means to get a place. It usually requires a history of taking care of a house or apartment, the required deposits and some promise of future income before someone will offer you a place. Ted did this very special thing for me at a time when he didn't even know me. I will always be grateful to him and his wife.

My then ex-wife's (the plaintiff) uncle owned a sign shop nearby and made some signs for me to solicit residential re-roof work (now that I had a phone number). I nailed them around the area on telephone poles and other places that got a lot of traffic. Before long the phone started ringing. I began bidding on and getting roofing jobs. I had no truck or means of hauling debris or materials. But I knew by doing roof work I could order dumpsters delivered to the job site for tearing off the old roofs and the supply places would roof-top deliver all the materials. All I needed was a ladder and some hand tools. Hard work but I could just show up, do the job and get paid when I was finished. In a few months, I was able to re-activate my contractors' license and moved towards doing some larger jobs.

Another significant requirement of my probation was to attend and actively participate in therapy. The County offered a group program which barely met that requirement. The laws and funding made available for sex-related crime counseling was directed almost entirely toward the victim(s) and little for the perpetrator(s). I realize all victims and their immediate family members need counseling to come to terms with such crimes. My situation was no different. The problem with the program I attended was, due to budget restrictions, the County had all the victims and all the offenders meet in the same facility at the same time. Think about that! The victims knew that their offenders were *just down the hallway.* In my particular case, the program had to seek an exception to my in force restraining order to allow me to attend. I got the feeling their program was a joke. All the counselors were women and extremely biased. They gave little concern and no respect toward the offender(s). They gave us 'homework' which was ridiculous like continuously going over "family of origin issues" re-starting back at square one each time a new person showed up. None of what we were doing was working at any of the core reasons as to why we molested or offended. It was all for the counseling service program to document an effort had been made and it was entitled to be compensated.

In the beginning of this book, I brought to your attention the fact that I had a history of making poor decisions. I hope by now you can certainly see that a change was in order. To that point even I hadn't grasped how much I needed to change **how** I approached my decision-making. I *needed* counseling. *That* counseling wasn't working. I had a problem.

I had lost respect for the program and started showing up and just going through the paces. The counselors bickered among themselves as to who "got stuck" with the offenders' (men's) group. It was just a travesty. They wasted a golden opportunity to help some people understand themselves and make genuinely positive changes in the directions their lives were heading. THEY JUST BLEW IT. But to them I was just another perp (perpetrator).

Time went on. I was a faithful attendee at every meeting. I wasn't learning a thing. All I was doing was the homework and participating in the group discussions. That group seemed to play to the lowest common denominator reaching down to the dumbest one in the group. Since it was an open group people came into and out of the group all the time. It became a common routine of a handful of things to rehash every time somebody new showed up. All that really seemed to be accomplished was another offender was off the streets and getting "counseling." So probation must be working. The counselors were getting paid.

By the end of the summer of 1994 I was still living at the same place I was caretaking. My son Mark came to live with me. That was a big deal because it took great effort for the probation department to allow my son to live with his 'offender' father. He was sixteen. His mother and he weren't getting along. So I welcomed having him stay with me. Together we converted a detached enclosed garage across a breezeway from my humble quarters into a room for Mark, a place for his friends to come over and "hang out."

Due to the fact that I was getting no help in counseling as to why I had made bad choices again I made a *really* bad move. I had for about a year been dating a woman ten years younger than I. It was approaching her birthday. I wanted to do something special for her but lacked the money. A fellow contractor at the last minute on a Friday afternoon invited me to go to Reno for a weekend as a consultant and stay at a luxury hotel complements of the casino-hotel he was working on.

One of the restrictions of my probation was not to leave the state without securing permission in advance. It's a standard probation restriction because if a probationer leaves the state they go outside the states' jurisdiction and control. Getting permission is usually no big deal as long as you sign allowing the state to come get you or have you brought back if you don't return as promised. Well, two things came into play there. First, I needed permission to go. Second, my son was still a minor about three months away from his eighteenth birthday. I tried to contact my probation officer most of that afternoon. I wanted to leave the next morning. Unable to connect, since it was Friday I figured he had taken off early. I had on prior occasions during probation gone out of the State (even to Mexico once) but always had permission in advance. So I knew probation didn't have any problem with me leaving. After several attempts to secure permission and feeling confident in my relationship with my officer, I elected to leave for the weekend without getting the required permission. We had a really great time. No one was harmed in any way.

A few weeks went by. Mark inadvertently told his mother (the plaintiff) during a casual conversation that I had gone away with my girlfriend on the weekend in question. She probed him further to find out exactly where I'd gone. She made a "big deal" out of him being left at home alone. Mark wasn't aware it was a potential violation for me to leave the State. He only thought she was bitching about me leaving him alone. He was even somewhat offended that his mother was giving him crap about being "unsupervised." Mark told her to forget it and mind her own business. It wasn't like he was on good terms with her after having to come and live with me. He asserted he was capable of taking care of himself. Besides what seventeen and three-quarters year old wouldn't jump at the chance to have a weekend home alone without any parent around? Mark was working, driving and going to school very responsibly without the need of my supervision or anyone else's. He was a grown young man. I was proud of him and trusted his judgment. I didn't see any need to tell Mark not to discuss my business with his mother. I failed to realize if she found out I had left the State without the required permission she could stir up the shit (her specialty). I also underestimated the anger and bitterness she still harbored. *That was just the bullet she needed*. She contacted my probation officer and complained that I had "left our MINOR son home alone the entire weekend." The probation officer asked her where I'd gone. She *gladly* told him **Reno** (out of the State), most likely with a big smile on her face.

A few days went by. I received a call from my probation officer asking, "Did you go out of State without permission?"(Not "did you leave your son home alone?") Without hesitation I denied I had left the State. A few days went by and I felt guilty about lying to my probation officer. He had treated me well considering the circumstances and this was no way to treat him with dishonesty. I should have just admitted to him what had happened and trusted his judgment. So I called and made an appointment to go see him in person hoping to make things right. Meanwhile, motivated by Nancy's insistent demand they "do something about this," and I suspect a little investigative help as to exactly where in Reno I'd gone my P.O. contacted the hotel where I had stayed. Even though everything was complementary, I had signed for all the restaurant tickets and room service etc. He had copies of all the receipts bearing my signature as evidence.

When I arrived I was asked to wait in a separate room. About an hour went by and instead of seeing my probation officer, two uniformed officers showed up from XXXXX County, arrested and transported me back to the county jail for a violation of probation (VOP)[17]. In the Penal system that is treated as a completely new offense.

At the time of my second arrest, I had struggled to get some footing under my business and was just completing

---

[17] Formal (felony)Probation Violation; www.california-criminal-lawyer.com/lawyer-attorney-1784431.html

a new contract home for a family in Sacramento. They had no knowledge I was a *registered sex offender.* My probation officer had counseled me it wasn't necessary to divulge that information just to build a house. Suddenly I was in jail again trying to figure out how to get bailed out and finish their home. I was out in a few days but by then the family found out I was a *sex offender* and **terminated** my contract. There was a question as to whether they could do that legally, but that was a civil matter and I had bigger problems to contend with. Not being able to complete that house cost me over $30,000 dollars which was everything to me at the time. There I was broke again after making *another dumb decision* thinking I could bend the rules "just a little."

My new attorney and I showed up at the court hearing without a defense. I was absolutely guilty of violating my probation by going out of state without advance permission. We were going to rely on the judge's wisdom in determining the next course of punishment. The prosecutor brought in the probation officer to establish the facts of my violation. He also requested my program counselors to be there seeking their input on deciding what should happen next. An argument broke out in court when those Femi-Nazi bitches tried to convince the judge I wasn't fit to remain on probation. According to them I should go straight to prison. My attorney vigorously fought back. The argument got hotter. It erupted into a big shouting match between my pit-bull attorney and those men-hating-masquerading-counselors who were hell bent on seeing to it that I paid. I didn't think they were ready for my attorney to jump on them the way he did. He lit into them shredding their program and they stumbled and fumbled to defend their position. They showed-up thinking they could just send me away not expecting a fight. But my attorney and I weren't gonna let 'em treat me like some typical knuckle-dragging-bottom-feeding perp. Finally, the judge interrupted the proceedings and ordered everyone except me, the clerks and the marshal into his chambers to "continue the discussion". He wanted it off the record so the shit could really fly. His chambers were just through a nearby door. As everybody raised up my attorney turned to me firmly saying, "don't ask; sit still and shut up." Heading to the judge's cave while obviously fuming one of those "therapists" glanced over towards me with contentious eyes and a smirk. I felt like flipping her off but I nervously sat there motionless. The door closed. It became real quiet for a few minutes. Then all I could hear was my attorney's voice shouting above everyone else's though I couldn't make out a word of what he was saying. I heard what sounded like fist pounding on a table. The clerks and marshal waiting in the court room with me were getting nervous. Then just as fast as everything had escalated into a yelling match it stopped. Silence returned. A few more moments passed and the door slowly opened. Everybody acting professionally calmly came back and took their places. The judge was last to re-enter. The court staff relaxed. My heartbeat was racing and my palms sweating in anticipation of the next move. I braced myself. I could barely breathe. The judge sat down on the bench and paused. He turned looking directly at me and asked if I was guilty. I lowered my head. My heart was pounding in my chest. With shallow breathing and a trembling voice said, "Yes your honor." "Very well," he responded. Again he paused riffling through a stack of papers making some notes. He turned toward me and looked up making eye contact again as he accepted my guilty plea. He declared, "Your probation is revoked." My heart dropped. All hope vanished. Part of me wanted to cry but I had to man-up and take my lumps. It seemed like time stood still. I instantly felt a chill as if my blood had gone cold and was rushing out of my body. I knew I was all done. He looked around the court room and stared back at me with piercing eyes hesitated for a moment then said, "I am going to offer you a chance back at probation with some added conditions." WHAT? Startled I whispered to my attorney "WHAT did he say?" As I looked at my attorney he snapped back at me "shut-up". Then it hit me what the judge had just said my heart started to pump again. He continued, "I am going to reinstate your probation but **I don't want to see you back here in my courtroom again** or I'll have little choice but to send you to prison." Pausing again and looking irritated he took a deep breath then raising his voice sternly said, "Do you understand me?" Humbly I said, "Yes your honor," nodding in appreciation, "you won't see back here." Then unbelievably after another moment passed he ordered me out of the counseling program. He told me to report to my former psychiatrist for treatment, the same psychiatrist who deemed me suitable for probation in the first place. Wow no more of those "ball-busting, man-hating phony counselors. The judge slammed the gavel and said "next case." I was free to go!

Halleluiah! I felt so relieved. Leaving the court that day I was totally thankful I had been given another chance. I was grateful to God, even though I wasn't relying on Him as much as I should have been, I had another chance. In addition to the new restrictions, I had to serve a county jail sentence of about eight months for the violation but given the alternative that wasn't going to be a problem. As we left the courthouse my attorney remarked with a big Cheshire cat grin on his face, "I knew at least one of us was going home today." I glared back at him but only one of us was laughing.

15

About a month passed before I had to surrender and serve my *second* term in the county jail. Facing the time wasn't nearly as scary as the unknown first time. I was as prepared as I could be when I got there. Relying on my limited past experience I did a few things that would make this time pass by a little easier. The jail had a policy that outside publications were allowed if they came directly from the publisher. An inmate could receive books, magazines, and newspapers as long as they were delivered directly from the source. Being aware of that policy I subscribed to the Sacramento daily newspaper paying in advance so the jail personnel were obligated to bring me the newspaper. I also placed a significant amount of money "on the books" at the jail that inmates used to purchase items while in custody.

The first week I spent in a solitary cell. That was to "protect" me as my previous underlying offence was a sex-related crime and I had formerly worked for a law enforcement agency. I requested a visit by the jail staff person in charge of determining where I'd spend the next eight months and what I would be able to do. He was quite concerned. In society in general it seems there is nothing more loathed than a *sex offender.* But in the jail environment its *magnified.* There are no distinctions in the severity of a crime but sex crimes retained their own special distinction. Any inmate that committed a sex offense against a minor or child, if discovered by the general population, resulted in labeling that inmate a 'baby rapist' and placed him in great danger.

The main jail consisted of a high security locked-up group, mostly those who were charged with a crime and waiting disposition from the court. Once a sentence was determined, they were processed to either the State prison (if longer than a year) or to a less secure "trustee" situation. The jail was always overcrowded so the staff was looking for **any** way to process out low risk inmates. They wanted to move me to a less secure barracks situation as soon as they could and assign me a job during my stay. In order to accomplish that, they decided to give me an alibi story for my crime and sentence. The outside public seems to be interested in **what** crimes the inmates commit more so then on the inside. The inmates are mostly concerned about release dates and not so much about reason(s) anyone is there. But in the event another inmate asked me why I was doing time, I was to tell him I was a contractor and had passed bad checks. That avoided disclosing the **real** reason and kept me somewhat out of danger.

Everything inside the barracks and all the things associated with jail were geared around manipulation. A sort of 'pecking order' developed among the inmates. I was ten-to-fifteen-years-older than most of the young punks in the barracks so I took advantage of my age to attract power. Since I was a building contractor on the outside I was assigned a special task for the County. Every morning a worker from their facilities department came to the jail and specifically 'checked me out' of the barracks. I worked for him throughout the day. Then he returned me to the jail when we were done, usually just prior to dinner. After doing small construction jobs for a short time the word must have gotten back to his bosses that I had a high level of skills so I was put in charge of totally remodeling the County's welfare offices. The worker that I was assigned to was technically responsible for the project; but it was well over his head. Recognizing my abilities they made me the project manager or "stand-in contractor" with him "supervising" me. The entire county welfare office staff was temporarily relocated to another location so the remodel work could take place. I was allowed to select a crew from the barracks to help with the work. That made me "THE MAN" inside the barracks. If someone wanted to get released on a work detail for the day he'd better be on my good side so I'd recommend his help. We did everything associated with construction. We built walls, re-wired electrical and communication cables, dry-walled, painted, laid flooring and everything else needed to completely remodel and upgrade their offices. I estimated all that work saved the county approximately $500,000 in labor alone. I did it for a single can of soda each day. Because of my efforts the various County department heads recognizing my exemplary work offered letters to the jail recommending they consider me for an early release. After all, I'd saved the county a truckload of money.

During my confinement I sort of ran things inside. I even taught the younger guys math skills so they could pass their GED[18] test before they left. I tried to help out the staff as well.

---

[18] GED General Education Development—Attained high school level academic skills; wikipedia.org/wiki/General_Educational_Development

Smoking was absolutely not allowed in jail. In fact it was the number one taboo. Little did they know I ran a cigarette smuggling operation on the side. And I don't even smoke. One of the side benefits of being able to work away from the jail was I had access to a phone to make private calls that weren't monitored. What I did was acquire cartons of cigarettes through contacts on the outside. The jail gave each inmate a sack lunch in the morning to take to their job. The lunch always included a sandwich in a zip-lock plastic bag. My "crew" re-used the plastic bags to "conceal" the cigarettes in order to get by the guards inspection upon their return to the barracks. I'll leave you to your own imagination as to where they concealed them. Once smuggled inside I had my guys 'sell' them. The medium of exchange was candy bars. And candy bars could only be acquired from the commissary paid for by money "on the books", either brought by the inmate initially or added by someone from the outside. Outside money was then credited to an inmate's account to be used while he was inside. Some of the less fortunate inmates had no money "on the 'books" and were left out, unable to buy snacks from the weekly commissary. Some of these guys were on my "crew." The price for cigarettes on a weekday was a candy bar, on week-ends two candy bars per cigarette. The 'smugglers' would handle distribution and the purchasers would drop their 'payments' into my locker. That way I never had any cigarettes in my possession. I would then take all the candy bars and see to it every week each of the 'welfare' inmates (no money "on the books") got at least one candy bar in their 'welfare bag' provided by the jail (which usually had a few stamps or envelopes with maybe soap or tooth paste). Word got around that all of these "treats" were coming from me. So I was solidified as "THE MAN" inside the barracks. Even the jail personnel thought I was doing a commendable thing by *sharing* and since I was an older inmate the younger guys I helped looked up to me as a mentor.

The point of this story is to remind you I was in custody because of my bad choices. And the system was reinforcing my manipulating behavior by itself using me and then allowing me to operate as I did. You would think that would be the last thing they would want to do to with a *sex offender!* Put me in charge, groom guys to do certain construction tasks, (and smuggle) manipulate events to my advantage and decide who got privileges. Brilliant! So much for the rehabilitation.

While in custody I was confronted with a situation that dramatically challenged my character. I was understandably angry at my ex-wife for her part in my being there. One day I was contacted away from the jail (while I was working at the Welfare office) by Nancy's sister-in-law who was married to Nancy's younger brother. She had her own reasons for being upset at both Nancy and Nancy's older brother—the bastard that molested Nancy. Her marriage to Nancy's younger brother was heading on the rocks. She offered to take a loaded handgun that her husband had borrowed from his brother (the cop) and place it along with some drugs in small plastic 'for sale' bags inside a shoebox under Nancy's car-seat. Then snitch her to the cops. My 'ex' would have been found with salable drugs and a loaded handgun registered to her older brother the cop. You know the old what-goes-around-comes-around. A super payback for my being in jail. It was an enticing temptation, like killing two birds with one stone both her and her brother. I would have a perfect alibi being in custody. Nancy would be busted and lose her cherished State job. Who knows what would have happened to her brother. I was very tempted. But I had not *completely* lost my mind. Besides, my youngest daughter was still under-age and living with her mother. So I passed on that delicious 'opportunity.'

The customary policy of releasing jail inmates was to let them go any time after dinner on the day prior to their actual release date as long as they had a ride. Otherwise the jail would have to release them right at midnight when the calendar changed. Most guys were being released from a month to a few weeks early to ease overcrowding. The drug offenders were the first to go. They knew they would be the first to return. The DUI guys next, then any first timers. When my release date finally arrived, I was let go at 12:01 am on the day I was to be released, in the middle of the night and not one minute earlier as I had been promised in spite of any letters or other recommendations, without a ride. Have a nice day (night) *sex offender* **(asshole).** And don't come back. Point well made.

16

Upon my release from custody the second time, I went (as ordered by the court) to the psychiatrist's office and entered his program. **That would prove to be the most positive thing that happened during my entire time on probation**. In fact, it became life-changing.

Dr. Johns ran a therapy group of male offenders that met at his office for an hour each week. During those sessions he concentrated on each individual's participation in the 'group discussion.' Then during the week, at different times, he scheduled separate one-on-one appointments to address each person's particular needs. In the beginning I was a little skeptical based on my prior experience with group counseling. I didn't want to waste my time again doing a bunch of mundane exercises. But I soon discovered his program was much different.

The group I was in was comprised entirely of professional men. It included teachers, a lawyer, a dentist, two social workers, a pastor, a physician, and even a city councilman.

Some of us were there as a part of court ordered treatment (like me), the rest as either diversion from being prosecuted or a condition to not having a license revoked. Finally! I was among intelligent people who could carry on meaningful conversations. What we all had in common was our *lost respect* in the community. We had become saddled with the burdens of shame and scorn that came with being (or accused of being) a *sex offender*.

One purpose of the group was to restore our dignity and self-respect, if only among ourselves. We explored all the different kinds of mistakes we had made. We held each other accountable. We did not allow anyone to minimize his situation. Instead we focused on being fully responsible for our actions and/or our victims. We learned to understand what we had done and why. Then we used our time to develop new, more appropriate behaviors to avoid repeating those past poor choices. It was a place to unload and share our burdens. We listened intently, cried deeply and opened up our inner selves. In that place there was no room to guard our "images" or protect any false projections of who we wanted others to think we were. We became real, honest and *totally exposed*. And we bonded together in support of each other.

Those sessions, together with the individual appointments, opened me up to a whole new way of seeing myself and gave me a starting place to begin putting myself back together. I embraced the opportunity.

For those of you who have never been involved in group counseling or any form of therapy, the first challenge is to relax and feel safe. People have to have a sense of trust in order to share their inner selves. At first most people naturally are apprehensive, defensive or skeptical. They keep their guard up until they feel accepted and know its okay to be candid. Once that is accomplished they can open up and be vulnerable. That's when treatment starts.

Our group had a unique way of welcoming new members. Whenever one showed up for his first meeting we would all go into a pre-arranged game of playing 'who's the therapist?' Dr. Johns would just be part of the group's circle. He was blind, wore no sunglasses and had each eye "aimed" in a different direction. With that his casual appearance and seeming indifference he was hardly ever considered the therapist. Each of us took a shot at 'acting' like the group leader while the rest observed how perplexed the new person became. By the end of the session we would confess what we were up to and all have a good laugh. *Welcome to the "group."* A side benefit of this was the doctor could "observe" the new guy as if he was a peer. That usually allowed the new member to feel relaxed, accepted and safe. It accelerated his trust and opened him up to sharing.

Consider now the *process* of making choices. Many of us don't consciously evaluate the choices we make. We tend to act based on our past experiences influenced in part by our families, childhoods, education, religion or other things we've been exposed to. We've been **taught**. I've attempted to show you how I simply made choices as I'd been taught through example without really thinking. *I did as I was told or shown.* Don't be so sure everything you think or believe is as accurate as you may want it to be. I'll give you a few examples to illustrate.

I was raised in the public school system in California. I was *taught* we live in a democracy. Most of us believe just that. However, actually we don't. Instead we live in a Constitutional Republic.[19] Democracy is rule by majority or mob rule, a

---

[19] www.stopthenorthamericanunion.com/NotDemocracy.html

"mobocracy."[20] In a Constitutional Republic one may acquit a person by not voting guilty in a jury thereby rendering the other eleven guilty votes meaningless. That gives the individual a lot of power even power **over** the government. If you think I'm wrong, study 'Prohibition' (1920 to 1933)[21] and why it was reversed. Juries used nullification[22] to send messages to prosecutors about misplaced enforcement priorities and harassing or abusive prosecutions. That contributed to the eventual repeal of prohibition. The government couldn't get convictions. No matter how hard they tried and no matter how guilty the offender was they just couldn't get twelve people to agree that drinking alcohol was wrong. Juries decided the **law was wrong**. Eventually the government gave in and decided to regulate booze and put a tax on it. First it was wrong; then it was okay to regulate and make revenue from it. A Constitutional Republic at work. (You didn't learn that in government class!)

Another example of just accepting without giving it much thought happens in California. California has a state income tax. We pay our taxes to the **Franchise Tax Board**. Ever

---

[20] www.merriam-webster.com/dictionary/mobocracy
[21] www.historicpatterson.org/Exhibits/ExhProhibition.php
[22] www.legallad.quickanddirtytips.com/legal-jury-nullification.aspx

wonder why it's called that? The fact is the State considers everyone living in California a **franchisee** of the State. That is, every time a person asks the State for a "privilege," such as a driver's, marriage, or fishing license, he/she obligates himself/herself to the state as a franchisee. This asking for a "privilege" is an exchange or surrender of one's *sovereign* right as a citizen. We actually *subjugate* ourselves to the government rather than being *above* the government. One doesn't need a *license* (permission) to travel on our highways. But one does need a license to *operate* a motorized vehicle on the State's property. Two people may be joined together under God. But in order to enjoy the legal benefits the State grants married people, they need to ask for a license. We ask. The government grants and *takes.* How's that make you feel? This may be quite a surprise to some of you. As a sovereign citizen you **already have** all of your rights. You only need "constitutional rights" when the government is coming after (charges) you. We give up our sovereignty much too easily.

My point is that some things we've been taught are not necessarily a complete picture. In our childhood we may not have gotten all the pieces to the puzzle or may have picked up some defective pieces. In light of this I'd like you to consider what makes you tick. What defines you? What is the basis of your decision-making? What are your preconceived biases? Where do they come from? Do you "think" before you act? What are your "automatic" responses? Have you just "accepted" the things you've been taught? Are you "programmed?" Are **you** running your life or is **it** running you? This very eye-opener caused me to stop and consider everything I had previously believed and trusted. This was the start to the unraveling of my inner self. I had a chance to inspect every aspect of my very foundation. By sorting out the "bad" pieces or filling in the holes I might re-build a more solid base. Better choices could be made.

17

"Hello. Who are you?" the doctor asked me during the first of many one-on-one sessions intermixed with my group counseling.

I rolled into that meeting with an attitude similar to starting a new college class. Just give me the assignments. I'd jump through the hoops and knockout an "A" and that would be that. Things were different there as we talked about my previous experience in the County program so he could gauge the level of misinformation I had received and establish a baseline to work with. At the end of our first session, his "assignment" was for me to go home and return with a list of 'who I was.'

The following week I showed up with a list on a sheet of paper feeling pretty good. I had completed the homework and was ready to show him how smart I was. I read it to him. When I finished he asked me to give it to him. He promptly wadded it up and tossed it into the garbage can. Turning to me he said, "I want you to go home and come back next week and tell me who you are." I was puzzled. I said, "It was all on the list Doc". So I retrieved it and we reviewed. On my written list were things such as: I was a dad. I was a contractor. I was a son, a brother, an uncle, even an offender. And so it resembled a poorly constructed obituary. Then he said something very profound, a key to my treatment. He said, "I'm not interested in your standing with your family or work. I don't want to know how you're related to others or what your career or profession is. I want to know **who** you are." He told me to go home, take a tablet into the bathroom, shut the door and look directly into the mirror. "Look at yourself, study and write down **who** you are." Okay. I was a little down as I wasn't used to failing an assignment. I thought that shouldn't be too difficult and left.

During the next few days, I considered what the doctor had said. It bugged me. Finally, after some procrastination, I said to myself, "Okay. Stop avoiding this and get it done." So I grabbed my pen, notepad and a chair. I headed to the bathroom. Closing the door, I turned and looked at myself like I was about to shave. No big deal. I took the pen to write and a deep breath to relax. I said to myself, "Come on. This isn't hard." I stared at myself and I focused on my eyes, gazing into the "window of my soul." I was startled to see emptiness. It seemed there was nothing there. I stared in the mirror. Minutes passed. Then nearly an hour. I felt blocked. I concentrated and still nothing on the paper. Then a draft of cold air crawled over me and sent chills up my spine. I felt hopeless. I lost it. I broke down sobbing. For the first time in more than I could remember, tears streamed down my face. I was out of control, crying. Minutes more passed. I *felt* the loss. Then my sobbing slowed and breathing returned to normal. I felt as if a dam had broken and lifted this immense pressure off me. At the same time same I felt despair for not having anything to write down. Regaining some composure I glanced back at the mirror. "We really need to get in touch. We have lots of work to do".

I returned to the doctor with a blank report. He wasn't surprised. Then together we started the journey to unravel why I was disconnected from my inner self. Throughout those next few months I was able to take everything I had learned, accepted, believed and counted on, scatter all of it out on the table and start sorting through it. It was like a spring cleaning of my soul. As a contractor I knew all the tricks to remodel a house but I needed to remodel my inner being. I began stripping out the garbage that had *interrupted* my life for years. Then started putting back the things I wanted to keep. Nobody else had to approve or disapprove regarding **who I thought I was**. I was free to explore myself to find out who I really was. What made me tick, turn on, create, react, and the big one—make decisions for myself not because of anyone else, my upbringing or my background.

I faced myself many times in the bathroom mirror. I began to write and write. I discovered myself. Sure, I was a father because I had children. I had been a husband because I had been married and had an ex-wife to prove it. I was a son to my mother and a brother to my siblings because I was born into my family. But that was **not** *who I was*. I discovered I am a feeling, loving, sharing, generous person with a certain level of intelligence. I'm ambitious, competitive, outgoing, creative, and dependable. I am caring, considerate and never take advantage of someone else's weakness. I go out of my way to help others. I empathize with people in their struggles and rejoice and celebrate their joys. I relate to people and their circumstances. I do things to ease the road they travel. It makes mine more interesting. I really know where the blessings are now and where they come from. God willing, every now and then, I get to *be* a blessing to somebody else and that's an added blessing to me. I could write a whole other book on who I am now. But I will spare you all that. I am no longer a scared wounded little boy under-nurtured, disillusioned, lacking appreciation or validation running around in the body of a grown man. Instead I'm a grown man with a happy little boy running around excited to be alive in this middle-aged, overweight body of a "prince." I know who I am. I'm a pretty cool guy content with myself and frustrated with a system that requires me to continually pay for an "ancient" offense. I have learned new purpose, and found new joy and energy in living.

18

I learned many things about myself beyond *who I was* during those sessions with the doctor. The most impacting one was the jolting discovery of a single core issue that changed everything. Once I understood its tremendous destructive power, I was without excuse for not changing. The demon that had me was my **internalized shame**.

I had never before understood what shame was. I learned in itself shame is not bad. It is a normal human emotion. The doctor explained to me it was necessary to feel shame to be truly human. But there actually were different kinds of shame, healthy as well as destructive. Healthy shame he said, "Keeps us in our human boundaries. It reminds us of our limits." The other kind of shame, destructive shame, he called **toxic.** Dr. Johns recommended I study a book by John Bradshaw, "Healing the Shame That Binds You." In that book I found the keys to why I was *disconnected* from my inner self. I learned **why** I didn't know who I was.

The following excerpt from John Bradshaw's book describes my experience to the letter. I encourage you to *s l o w   d o w n* and read each line to consider its' impact and power to destroy.

"Shame was the unconscious demon I had never acknowledged . . . . is one of the major destructive forces in all human life . . . . it can be transformed into shame as a state of being . . . . it takes over one's whole identity. To have shame as an identity is to believe that one's being is flawed.

He goes on to say that this toxic shame *"takes over one's whole identity . . . .* continuing once it is *"transformed into an identity it becomes dehumanizing . . . . it necessitates a cover-up . . . . a false self . . . . the real self ceasing to be an authentic human being.* Concluding, *toxic shame is the greatest form of **learned domestic violence** there is. It destroys human life . . . . it's everywhere. Toxic shame is cunning, powerful and baffling. Its power resides in its darkness and secretiveness."*[23]

---

[23] 1988 Health HEALING THE SHAME THAT BINDS YOU, John E. Bradshaw Communication, Inc. HCI, Deerfield, Florida

I studied Bradshaw's book intently. In the first part, he exposed the many faces of toxic shame, its origins and cover-ups. He showed me how it created hopelessness and spiritual bankruptcy. In the second part, he offered every way he knew for reducing toxic shame and transforming it back into healthy shame. I discovered how the unhealthy shame I'd learned over many years when I was young carried into my adulthood and became a core component of my decision-making process. I learned ways to free myself from that *menacing enemy*. It was not an easy task.

As mentioned earlier, I thought I was raised in a "normal" family. But a more detailed, in-depth look into my childhood revealed areas of development that weren't exactly nurtured. By example I was taught to hide my true self. I "learned" to disconnect from my feelings and wasn't allowed to talk about them or any dreams I may have had. Crying was a weakness and showed vulnerability. Under his "command," I spent my energy defending what I did or didn't do or blaming someone else for anything "out of order" hoping to avoid *the belt*. As a result, I was shown less concern for expression and more concern for performance. I became a human *doing* rather than a human *being*.

In my childhood home there was a lot of bickering, pointing out flaws and picking on the weakest. I was the only left-handed one in a family of eight. Instead of celebrating my uniqueness I was teased and put down. It was a right-handed world. I was an alien and *flawed*. I also had a pronounced space between my two upper-front teeth which made me feel like I could never "smile" in a picture. I had allergies which made my eyes appear red most of the time. I was sent home from school by the nurse on a regular basis with *pink eye* only to be sent back with a doctor's note explaining my allergies. As a child I tried to think it was a day off from school. But it was more like an interruption of my parent's life to "have to take a kid to the doctor." I remember vividly how the other kids stared and pointed at me. They laughed and said, "Ooohh, don't get near him." They called me the "sickee" and nicknamed me "Bloodshot."

I strove to overcome my "defects" by working to get excellent grades in school and playing sports. I thought any mistakes I made only "confirmed" my flaws. I recall a number of times when I brought home a report card with mostly 'A's (maybe one or two 'B's) and was met with "you need to improve (the B's)" while one of my younger brothers brought home all

D's and was praised for just trying. I didn't feel validated. I was not listened to. I wasn't good enough. I don't recall one instance when I was asked what I was going to do when I grew up. No discussions of what field of study I'd pursue in college or what do you think about God or any other ideas. I do remember my parents talking with other adults about how we may or may not "turn out." I had no idea what "turn out" meant. So I had no foundation.

I grew into adulthood without having a lot of self-confidence. I've had to create "games" to be able to finish projects because as a child I never got the prize, trophy, or praise for any accomplishment. I feared finishing because the disappointing let down was like popping a balloon. As a contractor, I enjoyed the process of building houses. I felt validated and important during the building process but struggled putting the final finishing touches on them. I feared there would be no payoff, no profit. I wasn't worth it. Classic toxic shamed to my core. Then after the molestation, I couldn't trust myself either. What a miserable place to be. Shame had severed every emotional inner connection I had. I couldn't even connect to myself. That was why I cried when I couldn't define *who I was*. I loved my daughter and couldn't believe what I had done. Who the hell was this counterfeit being inside me? Shame was the number one emotion I experienced even before regret, blame or guilt. It didn't want to let go. It was always present. It had bound me to a point of immobility. Most of us have a healthy level of shame or a conscience. It's that little voice that reminds us we should have done something or treated someone differently and, as a result, we feel bad. I was her dad, the supposed trusted parent. *What a disappointment to both of us!*

From that moment on, I carried the shamed, permanently tattooed scares of my actions. When it became a public issue, the shame grew uncontrollably. It kept all my feelings suppressed. I was "on guard" from any further damage and emotionally shackled until the legal battles were decided. I became hyper-vigilant like an animal protecting itself from any outward attacks. I circled the wagons and setup watch.

Fortunately after going through deep valleys and then ordered to Dr. Johns treatment, I realized I'd been *given the opportunity* to have a safe place and a caring doctor to guide me to find my lost self and *reconnect* me inside. That counterfeit darkness had to go!

Today I'm a valuable and contributing member of society. It tries to label me, but I refuse to wear that jacket. Instead, I am a genuine person that is required by law to maintain myself on a list the "public" (who my father used to say is about 85% morons being lead by 15% idiots (politicians)) seems to believe will make them safer.

My grown children today have told me of their feelings of being abandoned when they were young. That wasn't from physical *absence* but physical *presence.* Their feelings were ignored by both their mother and me when we were physically there. For them that was much more crazy-making. I was there but watching a game in the same room instead of talking and playing with them. Their mother would never listen to them. All she heard was her own demons. My energy was consumed by being all the things I falsely thought I was, the husband I thought a husband should be. I was playing the father role making a living and working hard (like I was taught) which "justified" my excuse to rest and relax when I was home instead of attending to my kids. And I was the Sunday school teacher which would make me feel accepted and I was "acting" like a Christian. I internalized so much shame that I had over time substituted a "counterfeit self for my *authentic* self."[24]

The multi-generational toxic shame syndrome was intact. As I looked at the ways I ignored my children, I remember the days when the Marine was gone working many days on the railroad. It wasn't how long he was gone. It was more about how little time he spent with us kids when he was home. It really was about the QUALITY and not the QUANITY. Imagine how I felt when he would come home and watch the game but would never come see me play sports. I felt I was *worth-less* than his time, wasn't important enough for his attention. Little did I know in many of the same ways, I treated my children the same as I had been treated (*taught*) and made them feel the same way. *The beat goes on*.

I should give my parents a little break though. They were caught up in day-to-day survival providing for a large family. They were both products of that multi-generational shaming as well. They lacked the skills to communicate with each other. So neither could effectively do so with us kids. I referred to it in the beginning of this book as "the sins of the father." Most of their energy was consumed by tasks rather than affirming

---

[24] Bradshaw

their children. We didn't get a lot of emotional support. We weren't told how unique and valuable we were. We didn't receive outward signs of affection. Our identity suffered as a result of neglect which was also a part of the reason I couldn't define who I was. But that type of neglect wasn't something they consciously decided to do. Instead it was repeating something they experienced in their own upbringing.

My dad is gone now. But I have a very special love and appreciation for my mom. When I was in my thirties I took it upon myself to express my love for my mom. Being *verbal* was new for both of us. And she learned how to express her love to all her kids. Until a few years ago, she lived close by. I was privileged to spend hours over coffee hearing stories of the past. Together we'd laugh, sometimes uncontrollably. She is eighty-five-years-old and now lives with my sister about 800 miles away in another state. I have the opportunity to visit her often. She is a tough old gal and so cute. I count myself blessed for having her and we frequently remind each other how much we're loved.

19

At the time I took the plea bargain I felt I was under extreme duress. I went into court ready to fight the charges but had to give up that fight and accept a plea deal. I became so anxious under the pressure to make the deal, focusing only on staying out of prison that I didn't pay much attention to any of the other "bargained" requirements. I was extremely relieved when I was allowed to go on probation instead of prison and felt grateful to have a chance at redemption. Upon completing the initial jail term (as part of my probation), I made a commitment to do whatever the probation department requested. But my stubborn nature and track-record of bending the rules "just a little" had landed me back in jail after the Reno lie. Following my second jail term I was determined to comply and get through probation successfully. My attorney told me once I completed probation I would be "completely" free. I'd have to break another law to get into trouble again. So my goal was to get it done. At the time I took the deal I remember the plea conditions being: STAY OUT OF PRISON, do a bunch of other stuff, STAY OUT OF PRISON and oh by-the-way register, as if registering was no big deal, more like a formality than a condition. I had no idea what that meant. It was prior to 1994 and dramatic changes were ahead for registrants.

In the first part of probation I was considered "in custody" even though I got to go home at night after work at the "dirt shed" with the ankle monitor firmly attached. It was only after I completed the jail portion of my probation and fully released back into the community that I was required to comply with the registration law (Penal Code 290)[25]. Not knowing anything about the registry I decided to find out WHAT it was and HOW and WHO used it. I asked myself those questions to have a better understanding as to why I had to be on it. I thought since my "crime" was against my daughter why did I have to be on a public list, especially after Dr. Johns reported to the court that I posed a very low risk. Why did anyone besides law enforcement have to have my information unless it was actually a further punishment? It seemed to me if the judge, prosecutor and my doctor had agreed I wasn't dangerous enough to go to prison then the public was already safe.

---

[25] California Penal Code 290; www.law.onecle.com/california/penal/290.html

Most people, including myself back then, thought sex offender registries had only recently been created. According to the National Center for Missing and Exploited Children's website[26] before 1994 very few states required registration of *sex offenders*. It gives the reader the notion the government started tracking *sex offenders* in the 1990s. That is far from the case.

In 1930-31 during prohibition the country fell into the Great Depression. That climate spawned an increase in home-grown-domestic-terrorism called Mafia gangsters. Their kingpins wielded a lot of unrestrained power in places like Chicago and New York. Fearing a growing menace, the Los Angeles County District Attorney[27] proposed an ordinance to keep organized crime out of LA. His proposal became the "convict registration" ordinance[28] when passed by the county Supervisors in 1933. It required anyone convicted of *certain* crimes to register with the sheriff if they lived in or visited LA County for more than 5 days. That became the template for registering felons in the future. The City of Los Angeles

---

[26] www.missingkids.com

[27] Los Angeles County District Attorney Buron Fitts 1928-1940; www.en.wikipedia.org/wiki/Buron_Fitts

[28] www.solresearch.org/~SOLR/cache/gov/US/loc/CA-LA/Police/1934-AnRep.pdf

soon adopted the county ordinance. Other cities in California followed suit.

In 1940, responding to efforts by the local chapter of the Parent-Teacher Association (PTA), the City of Los Angeles[29] came up with a plan to take the "convict" registry and add "sex" crimes to it. Among the first *sex crimes* listed were:

1. "lewd or lascivious act" on or with a child under 14
2. "indecent exposure"
3. "Sexual Perversion" (participating in oral sex) between consenting adults.

Over a seven year period an ordinance designed to keep gangsters out of LA evolved into the first sex registry. Even though the County of LA started the convict registry, it was the City of LA that pushed the state to adopt its model for a statewide registry law.

In 1947 the California State Legislature added Section 290 to the Penal Code requiring anyone in the state who had been convicted of any of a "list" of particular sex crimes to register

---

[29] www.solresearch.org/~SOLR/cache/gov/US/loc/CA-LA/19330911-file4788.pdf

with local police. At that time the State added to the listed crimes requiring registration:

4. "rape of a non-wife female by force, threat, or guile"
5. "entice or trick a female into having sex"
6. "abduct female under 18 into prostitution without parents' permission"
7. "seduction" (promise of marriage for sex)
8. "infamous crimes against nature" (anal sex with mankind or animal).
9. "annoy or molest a child"
10. "incest" (marriage or fornication with too closely related)
11. "lewdly influencing a person under 21 to become delinquent."[30]

The list became a favorite tool of the police to harass "undesirables." In 1949 in response to widespread hysteria regarding homosexuals, the State added a new law of "lewd

---

[30] www.solresearch.org/~SOLR/cache/gov/US/st/CA/legis/code/Penal-1947-sex.pdf

vagrancy."[31] Between 1949 and 1953 the police used that vagrancy law over 95 percent of the time to "get the queers" or prosecute homosexuals which were almost exclusively men. Fortunately in 2003, The United States Supreme Court struck down all laws dealing with anal and oral sex between consenting adults.[32]

Whatever happened to the "gangster law?" In 1960 the California State Supreme Court ruled that the State legislature retained exclusive power to regulate crime and took away all local municipalities' jurisdiction to create lists or registries.[33] Following that ruling the "gangster" or "convict" registries were dissolved leaving only the state wide sex registry.

As of 2009, the "list" of registrable crimes for adults in California had grown from the original eleven to 169 offenses and juveniles have their own list of 61.[34]

It wasn't until the mid-1990's, when some highly publicized sexual assaults against children occured, that federal laws

---

[31] www.solresearch.org/~SOLR/rprt/bkgrd/origin.asp. Pg. 2 "Lewd and dissolute vagrancy laws were typically used in California and some other states to harass and arrest adult men seeking or engaging in consensual sexual activity with each other."

[32] www.supremecourt.gov/opinions/boundvolumes/539bv.pdf pg 558-Lawerence v. Texas

[33] www.lexisnexis.com/clients/CACourts/ Abbott v. City of Los Angeles, Feb. 26, 1960

[34] www.meganslaw.ca.gov/registration/offenses.aspx

(Megan's, Adam Walsh, etc.)[35] were enacted requiring all States to (1) track sex offenders and (2) make certain information **available to the public**. At that time, Congress began passing a series of statutes that collectively required states to strengthen their procedures for tracking *sex offenders*. The emphasis of Congress was to make a clear distinction between non-violent and violent, high-risk, predatory sex offenders. But the federal laws left it up to each state to craft the particulars of their own registries. States without a registry made efforts to classify or "tier" registrants by revealing only high risk or dangerous offenders' information for public disclosure.

California, already having a registry in place, adopted the federal mandates to disclose information to the public without any attempt to distinguish between high-risks, dangerous offenders and those who were non-violent. There were no tools to determine the risk level posed by any registrant. All sex offenders listed on the registry were due to Penal Code **mandates** following conviction.

Before public disclosure mandates from the federal government there wasn't a need to "classify" a registrant since

---

[35] www.childwelfare.gov/systemwide/laws_policies/federal/index.cfm?
event=federalLegislation.view Legis&id=81

the intended original use of the list was only to assist law enforcement in solving crimes. The original Bill establishing the registry in California in 1947 (AB1124) stated that any "statements, photographs and fingerprints herein required **shall not be open to inspection by the public** or by any person other than a regularly employed peace or other law enforcement officer."[36] However, any legislator who may have had the wisdom to see the potential problem(s) and the nerve to push to modify the registry prior to it becoming **public** would have been seen as "soft on crime" and become an easy political target. When the original California registration law was enacted, the "lifetime" requirement was "assumed" because the information had always been intended to remain **confidential** within law enforcement agencies. There was never any legislative discussion about the length of time to keep individuals on the list or that it introduced potentially high cost including administrative expenditures for monitoring and keeping the registry current and accurate. Keeping it up-to-date or current wasn't a critical concern and lack of accuracy carried no liability. Furthermore, any attempt to create "classes" of sex offenders would require

---

[36] www.solresearch.org/~SOLR/cache/gov/US/st/CA/legis/1947-legis-sex.pdf pg.14

costly case-by-case assessments. That would have involved developing new assessment tools, qualification standards and certifying professionals using the tools to determine an offender's "classification" and administrators managing the listings and training staff. All carried a very high price tag. So the legislature took the easy way out and elected to adopt federal disclosure mandates without first fixing the registry to retain only high and dangerous offenders. Instead it made the list one-size-fits-all with full disclosure. The unintended consequences of not modifying the registry have resulted in employment, education and housing discrimination and violence toward registrants that pose no moderate or high risk to public safety. The California law requires registration for **all** 169 adult and 61 juvenile offenses with few exceptions **for life**. Notification laws allow anyone worldwide online access to this information (except the registrant him/herself to verify its accuracy).[37]

Proponents of the sex offender registration and notification laws believe they protect the public in two ways. First, by providing police a list of likely suspects should a neighborhood

---

[37] www.meganslaw.ca.gov/disclaimer.aspx?lang=ENGLISH   See   disclaimer: Legal and illegal uses (Penal Code 290.46 subd. (h)(2).)

crime occur where a registrant lives. And second, parents have information enabling them to be vigilant in caring for their children by warning them to stay away from certain people. These advocates believe restrictions will set limits on the offenders' ability to have access to children to commit a new crime. This is a false and mistaken premise. There is little evidence these laws have reduced the threat of sexual abuse to children or others.

Abduction, rape and murder of a child by a stranger who has a previous sex offense conviction are extremely rare. Sex offender laws based on preventing the horrific crimes that inspired them offer no protection to children from the serious risk of abuse facing them by family members or acquaintances. People that children know and trust are responsible for over 90 percent of sex abuse crimes against them.[38]

Additionally, these laws are predicated on the assumption that most sex offenders will commit more sex crimes if given the chance. The facts simply don't support this. Recidivism rates for sex offenders are the lowest of any crime other

---

[38] http://childparenting.about.com/od/healthsafety/a/Myths-About-Child-Sex-Offenders.htm

than murder.[39] Typically murders aren't released to be able to re-offend.

The justifications used to promote tougher sex offender laws need a clear definition of what constitutes a *sexually violent predator* and a focus on the most dangerous offenders.[40] And that definition needs to fit the crime, not some vaguely "hidden" or misleading government definition.

People who have not committed any violent or coercive crimes are required to register as sex offenders and are subject to notification and residency restrictions (one size fits all). There are many examples of people who urinated in public, teenagers who had consensual sex with each other, adults who sold sex to other adults and kids who exposed themselves in pranks that have to register.[41]

The length of time to remain on the registry is excessive. California and other states have **lifetime** registration without consideration of the nature of the offense and lacking any assessment of the likelihood that a former offender continues to pose a threat. Nationwide the trend is to increase duration

---

[39] wikipedia.org/wiki/Sex_offender#Recidivism_rates
[40] www.rivcosafe.publishpath.com/summary-of-svp-law
[41] http://forums.plentyoffish.com/14545485datingPostpage6.aspx

even though the facts are sex offenders are less and less likely to re-offend the longer they live offense free.[42]

If sex offenders had to only register with law enforcement then consequences for them would be reduced significantly. But online registries "label" everyone with the same stigma or "scarlet letter." So in addition to having a sex offense in their past, by association with the most dangerous remain a risk in the public eye. Most state registries only list the law violation by code without giving any useful information about the actual conduct so the public assumes the worst. When I first registered I wasn't concerned beyond trusting law enforcement to keep my private information confidential. I wasn't very concerned about whether or not it was kept indefinitely (for life) because I knew I would never re-offend. But when people see my picture on the internet they assume that I am a pedophile. I have been called a baby rapist. I've had disgusting things left on my door for my wife (who I wasn't with at the time of my offense) to witness. I've had debris thrown about my yard and vehicle vandalism. What the registry doesn't tell people is I took a plea of a much more serious crime than the facts supported, completed therapy and probation, never went

---

[42] http://www.mendeley.com/research/sex-offender-recidivism-simple-question/

to prison and was determined by the judge and my doctor to pose little public threat. In California the website doesn't list the year or date when the offense happened leaving the requestor to assume it was recent not over twenty years ago. There is no mention of mine as a one-time conviction with a record of no other offenses, not even a traffic citation. My life has been pushed to the brink of ruin many times, not because I molested my daughter and not because I was convicted, but because my former clients and current neighbors, out of irrational fear, reacted to information on the internet.

In the fall of 2006 California adopted legislation to create the California Sex Offender Management Board (CASOMB).[43] According to the CASOMB website California has the largest number of registered sex offenders in the United States, the state has about 90,000, 68,000 of whom are in the community. The rest are incarcerated.[44] This large number is due to the overall population of the state, the length of time California has been registering sex offenders (since 1947), the length of time of registration (lifetime) and the large number of offenses which require mandatory not discretionary sex offender registration.

---

[43] http://law.onecle.com/california/penal/sec-9000-9003.html
[44] http://www.casomb.org/reports.htm pg. 50.

California remains one of the few states that have lifetime registration for all sex offenders.[45] The so-called upside to this allows the public to be aware of the majority of them living in their neighborhoods. The downside is that the public and law enforcement agencies (for which the registry was originally intended) have no way of differentiating between higher and lower risk offenders. In this one-size-fits-all system of registration, law enforcement cannot concentrate its scarce resources on close supervision of the more dangerous registrants or on those who are at higher risk of committing another sex crime. This has rendered the usefulness of the registry to little more than community chaos and vigilante activity. The system is broken.

The stated vision of CASOMB is "to decrease sexual victimization and increase community safety."[46] Their vision will be realized by addressing issues, concerns and problems related to community management of adult (they have no authority over juveniles) sex offenders by identifying and developing recommendations to improve policies and practices.

---

[45] http://www.casomb.org/reports.htm pg 50 California is one of only four states having lifetime registration. The others are Florida, Alabama and South Carolina.

[46] http://www.casomb.org/ Home page—Vision

Over the past four years they have assessed the current adult sex offender management practices and have recommended the following:

1. Not all California sex offenders **need to register for life** in order to safeguard the public and so a **risk-based system** of differentiated registration requirements should be created

2. Focusing resources on registering and monitoring **moderate** to **high risk** sex offenders makes a community safer than trying to monitor **all** offenders for life.

3. A sex offender's risk of re-offense should be one factor in determining the length of time the person must register as a sex offender and whether to post the offender on the internet. Other factors which should determine duration of registration and internet posting include:

   A. Whether the sex offense was violent

   B. Whether the sex offense was against a child

C. Whether the offender was convicted of a new sex offense or violent offense after the first sex offense

D. Whether the person was civilly committed as a sexually violent predator[47]

The CASOMB recommends that a revised system of registration be developed based largely on the level of danger and risk of reoffending, a case-by-case assessment of every offender. It recommends a three-tiered system, which will assign a tier level to each sex offender depending, in part, on individual risk assessment, history of violent convictions, and sexual offense recidivism. It also recommends that sex offenders in tier 2 and 3 be posted on the public Megan's Law Internet web site.[48]

According to CASOMB the most serious issue facing California today in the field of sex offender management is the dramatic increase in the number of sex offenders registered as transients.[49] Residence restrictions are ineffective and

---

[47] CASOMB Recommendation, January 2010 pg 51

[48] http://www.casomb.org/docs/CASOMB%20Report%20Jan%202010_Final%20Report.pdf pg 55.

[49] CASOMB Letter Regarding Chelsea's Law (AB 1844) pg 1

ridiculous. There is no evidence whatsoever that by restricting sex offenders from living near "where children gather" will protect children from sexual violence. A child molester who does offend again is as likely to victimize a child found far from his home as he is one who lives nearby. In spite of this, residency restrictions apply to all sex offenders regardless if their prior offense even **involved** children. The CASOMB has noted research shows sex offender offenders who live near schools or parks do not have a greater likelihood of re-offending. Therefore, residence restrictions should be limited to offenders who have committed violent sex offenses against children, sexually violent offenders, and repeat sex offenders.[50] In other words, residency should be a matter of individual assessment not a general, all-inclusive one-size-fits-all restriction but one based on risk.

The risk should be assessed on a case-by-case method for each convicted sex offender using proven tools that have predictive validity. Recently the California State Authorized Risk Assessment Tool for Sex Offenders committee (SARATSO), following years of study, has advised the Governor of a selection of assessment tools to implement in 2012. These

---

[50] CASOMB Letter Regarding Chelsea's Law (AB 1844) pg 1

tools will measure the risk of violent re-offense[51] as well as dynamic (changing)[52] risk factors for sex offenders while on parole or probation. Perhaps these same tools could be used to determine tier level of registration in the future should California modify its current lifetime requirement. Former offenders who have completed parole and probation and determined to be low risk for reoffending, verified by an individual assessment, should be released from the register requirement at some point. The period of time to be "listed" should vary from high, medium and low risk assessment with periodic review. Access to sex offenders' information should be exclusively limited to law enforcement (as the original registry intended).

The Adam Walsh Act requiring full public disclosure should be repealed entirely. There is little evidence that public disclosure increases public safety.

The CASOMB recommends to the State Legislature, Governor and citizenry as related to the implementation of the Adam Walsh Act **not to come into compliance.**[53] The

---

[51] http://www.cdcr.ca.gov/Parole/SARATSO_Committee/DOCS/SARATSO_ Letter_to_Gov_-_LSCMI.pdf

[52] http://www.cdcr.ca.gov/Parole/SARATSO_Committee/DOCS/SRA-FV_ Letter_to_Gov_2.25.11.pdf

[53] http://www.casomb.org/docs/Adam%20Walsh%20Position%20Paper.pdf Pg 1

potential cost of implementation (estimated $32 million)[54] far exceed the penalty in federal funding (estimated $2.1 million Justice Assistance Grants)[55] for non-compliance without any evidence that adopting the Act would promote public safety. At the very least states should enact laws allowing all registrants to appear before a panel of qualified professionals to review the requirement of law enforcement to **publicly release** their private information. Registrants should be able to present evidence of rehabilitation, change in situation, incapacitation (disability) and substantial time without re-offense in order to **terminate community notification** and **internet inclusion**. All States should only include information online for **high risk** offenders and for only as long as they remain high risk. Any information disclosed should contain enough to understand the nature of the offense and the registrants' risk level to re-offend, and be updated periodically.

No state should have residency restrictions that apply to whole classes of former offenders. Authorized residency restrictions should be limited to individual offenders as a condition of parole, probation or mandated supervision.

---

[54] Ibid, Pg 2
[55] Ibid, Pg 3

20

In the small city where I live there are 95 registered citizens.[56] Having talked with the local police officers, they have unofficially said they only have to be concerned with 2 or 3 "bad guys." The rest are a waste of time and the department's resources. When I press them to make a comment on the record they reluctantly refuse (to avoid the heat from "on-high"). I wish any of them could live in my shoes for a little while to see how unjust the registry is.

California's registry contains people that committed the crime of being sixteen with a girlfriend of sixteen (Romeo and Juliet laws). How about those of you who are old enough to remember streaking? They, too, today would have to register. One could also land on the list for viewing internet pornography even if it was sent by someone else. And ladies, you can't have sex toy parties hawking vibrators to your friends or other such naughty stuff, especially if it's in close proximity to a school.

---

[56] Confirmed by the local Police Department—due to my desire to remain anonymous at this time I am not disclosing my city of residence

174

Amazingly, there are still statutes that any number of women living together constitutes a brothel! I wouldn't be surprised if being a sorority sister could land you on the same registry as Richard Allen Davis[57], the low-life-bottom-feeding-multiple-convicted-punk that abducted and murdered Polly Klaas[58].

In Georgia recently, a twenty-four-year-old man was arrested for wearing pants low enough to expose his boxers while riding his bicycle. He violated the city's ban on "baggy" pants.[59] Look out ladies you could be next. In Yakima, Washington a new city ordinance banning visible "cleavage of the buttocks" is in place. So girls beware. If your thong is showing and a child 14 or under sees it, up to one year in jail and registered.[60] Don't even think about breast-feeding in public. So riding your bicycle with your boxers showing or having a thong or "whale tail" showing or feeding your child in public could put you on a list for life allegedly "to protect the public." In 2007, a Florida state court prosecuted a sixteen-year-old girl for electronically sending (sexting)[61] nude

[57] http://en.wikipedia.org/wiki/Richard_Allen_Davis

[58] http://www.pollyklaas.org/about/pollys-story.html

[59] http://www.thepostsearchlight.com/news/2009/jan/13/baggy-pants-wearer-hitched/

[60] http://carnalnation.com/content/8342/4/crackdown-cleavage-buttocks

[61] SEXTING: This new form of social interaction has been coined "sexting." Sexting is the act of sending nude or sexually explicit photographs electronically,

pictures of herself to her seventeen-year-old boyfriend. The court charged her and her boyfriend with producing, directing, and promoting child pornography. These teens face severe lifetime punishment for unintentionally engaging in "criminal" behavior.[62] Teenagers today in California may well be advised taking and texting pictures between themselves (sexting) could very well stain the rest of their lives for having possession of child pornography.[63] This is not a laughing matter. No college. No place to live. And if the parents paid for the phone, well Mom and Dad welcome to the list.

A teenager asks his parent for birth control. Most parents may not like their child's activity but would consider this a sign of maturity and responsibility on the part of the child.

---

either through a picture text message using a cellular telephone or posting the picture on the Internet. While the idea of sexting may be shocking to adults, it is incredibly popular for teenagers across the United States. In fact, according to a study by the National Campaign to Prevent Teen Pregnancy, one in five teenagers (twenty percent) admit to participating in sexting. "What makes sexting so ripe for legal discussion is that it represents a social and technological phenomenon that has outstripped the law," as there is no consensus in the legal community as to the appropriate punishment for teenagers engaged in this behavior. Technological advancements and the resulting misuse by teens have forced prosecutors and legislatures across the country to strike a balance between protecting children from the harms of child pornography and the need to avoid imposing severe punishments on teenagers for unintentionally engaging in criminal behavior. http://www.noslang.com/sexting.php

[62] http://www.bu.edu/law/central/jd/organizations/journals/scitech/volume171/documents/Sherman_Web.pdf

[63] http://www.huffingtonpost.com/2011/07/12/california-sexting-law-sb_n_896352.html

But now parents that give their own children (under 18) any form of birth control can be prosecuted as accessory to sex crimes. In Mississippi, it is a crime for parents **not** to report to police that their kids are having sex. This law prohibits "the intentional *toleration* of a parent or caretaker of the child's sexual involvement with any other person."[64] Nowhere does it distinguish between sexual abuse and consensual encounters between teens. No wonder Mississippi ranks among the top five states as the highest teen pregnancy rate in the country![65] Imagine. You can't give your kid birth control. If she gets knocked-up and you knew she was sexually active, you could be prosecuted and have to register for life.

You think that's ridiculous? I even heard of a story of a father who was in a public place with his teenage daughter as she was eating a Popsicle. She was talking a lot and interrupting him. So he playfully shoved the Popsicle into her mouth when she didn't expect it. Her reaction caused alarm from bystanders that led to him being considered for charges of *penetrating his daughter with a foreign object!*

---

[64] http://billstatus.ls.state.ms.us/documents/2009/pdf/SB/2400-2499/SB2472PS.pdf
[65] http://www.guttmacher.org/pubs/USTPtrends.pdf pg13

Teachers look out. You could be next. In New York, a high school teacher was asked for advice on oral sex by one of her seventeen-year-old female students. She used words that, according to the school board, were "vulgar, obscene and disgusting." The words in question were "head job," "hand job," and "fellatio." The teacher, with over twenty years of experience and never having been in trouble before, found herself out of a job for responding to a question from her student.[66]

Welcome to *registered sex offender 101*.

I've heard talk recently on radio and television about America liberalizing social morality. But as long as teens are under attack for having sex and teachers and parents for talking about it or refusing to turn them in or providing responsible birth control, it seems we haven't progressed as far as some would like us to believe.

The Fifth Amendment of the Constitution of the United States of America protects individuals from double jeopardy[67] and guarantees that one will not be deprived of life, liberty or

---

[66] http://www.nbcnewyork.com/news/local/Sexy-Chat-With-Student-Earns-Teacher-Pink-

[67] http://legal-dictionary.thefreedictionary.com/fifth+amendment

property without due process of the law.[68] Article 1 Section 9 of the Constitution prohibits the Federal Government from enacting *ex post facto* laws and Article 1 Section 10 prohibits states from doing the same.[69] These rights should hold true for everyone including legal citizens, legal immigrants and law-abiding members of the community, as well as those who deviate from the law. However, it seems that they can be stripped "administratively" from those people that 'society' deems undesirable.

When an individual's behavior becomes criminal he becomes involved with the justice system. He is going to lose some of his rights until he is either cleared or serves his time and is released back into society. Once he has been granted release, shouldn't he once again be given the same rights and liberties that everyone else enjoys because he has lawfully re-paid his debt to society? Convicts are rarely able to recover their full rights once they've become involved with the Justice system. 'Ex-Cons' are severely stigmatized in a negative way. Some types of criminals are affected more than others. Due to some high-profile cases and subsequent legislation there is

---

[68] http://legal-dictionary.thefreedictionary.com/Due+Process+of+Law
[69] http://www.usconstitution.net/const.html

one group of ex-felon that is being deprived of more and more liberties with few advocates defending his/her rights. They are the **sex offenders**.

The public loves to hate *sex offenders*. And they are great political targets. The public also loves *sex offender* laws. But that doesn't mean any law dreamed up is going to solve the problem or make anyone safer. As a result, *sex offenders* have become the 21st century scapegoat for a generation of ambitious politicians and a vindictive society. Many people regard convicted *sex offenders* as the most disgusting, heinous type of human being. People do not want them living in their neighborhoods, being around their children or attending the same schools and functions as the rest of the community. So the question for many people is, what should we do with them? Do we allow them to live in our neighborhoods anonymously? Do we afford them the same rights as other ex-criminals? Along with the registration requirement, there is the advent of Civil Commitments[70] which amounts to imprisoning people for what they **might do in the future**. Clearly this is a violation of our citizens' rights. It's astounds me that when a person is charged with a sex crime the defendant is determined

---

[70] http://en.wikipedia.org/wiki/Involuntary_commitment

competent to stand trial. Then only after many years in prison found to have a mental abnormality and confined to a mental health facility **indefinitely! (Did he get the "mental abnormality" in prison?)**

How many of you think that all *sex offenders* are child predators? It should be clear by now, some are just bad dressers. Others just couldn't "hold it" and took a leak on the side of the road. Why is there no distinction between a violent child predator and a non-violent offender who has had no contact with children? Isn't it time to change these one-size-fits-all laws before more and more sexters[71] end up right next to Philip Garrido,[72] the nut-ball that abducted Jaycee Dugard,[73] and Brian David Mitchell,[74] the Utah freak that went "bat-shit" and kidnapped and tortured Elizabeth Smart.[75]

Let's suppose that there is a *murder offender list.* You have the misfortune of someone dying as a result of a traffic accident deemed to be your fault. You are sentenced to serve a period of time in jail, released and required to register. You

---

[71] http://www.reuters.com/article/2011/12/05/us-sexting-idUSTRE7B41HL20111205

[72] http://en.wikipedia.org/wiki/Kidnapping_of_Jaycee_Lee_Dugard

[73] http://en.wikipedia.org/wiki/Kidnapping_of_Jaycee_Lee_Dugard

[74] http://en.wikipedia.org/wiki/Brian_David_Mitchell

[75] http://en.wikipedia.org/wiki/Elizabeth_Smart_kidnapping

are placed on a list of *murderers*. You did not conspire to kill someone with your car. You didn't set out to cause a death. You were just driving along, missed a sign and bang! One horrific accident. One dead body. How do we know you can ever drive safely again? So off to the *murder offender list* you go. Right there with Charles Manson, Jeffery Dahmer, and Scott Peterson. MURDERER! The sad reality is that even if you did commit murder or vehicular manslaughter and served a sentence, after your release and a few years without any other convictions your record could be sealed. Nobody would be able to deny you an opportunity to work, get housing, etc. due to your being on a *murder offender list* which would show up in a 'background check.' There is a country song called, "If I shot her when I should have, I'd be out by now."[76] Amen.

As of 2006 the California Department of Corrections and Rehabilitation is required[77] to administer the Static 99[78] as a means to assess risk prior to a convict being released from prison back into society. What about all those on the list that were released *prior* to the availability of this tool? How about the ones who were never in prison but went straight to

---

[76] http://www.bored.com/countrysongtitles/

[77] http://www.cdcr.ca.gov/Parole/SARATSO_Committee/SARATSO.html

[78] http://www.static99.org/

probation (Like me—the majority)? ALL ARE INCLUDED ON THE LIST.

In my case, several laws were passed **after** my conviction and **after** I paid my debt to society that place even more restrictions on me and limit my liberties further. I consider this *double jeopardy*. They are also *ex post facto* (after the fact) and have been applied to me without due process.

Today in California there's a growing activist effort to push back against the increasing number of laws that restrict former sex offenders' citizen liberties by treating them as a whole class.[79] CASOMB has a clear understanding of the out-of-control dated policies which have resulted in the lop-sided, inflated registration numbers rendering the original intended use of the list ineffective. There is now a ratio of 1 in every 230 men in the state who are registered.[80] This has created a tremendous stress on already limited funds. The cost of maintaining the registry together with CASOMB's expert evaluation and courageous leadership in the state assembly has produced a new measure to create a three-tiered registry

---

[79] http://www.californiarsol.org/
[80] http://www.dof.ca.gov/research/demographic/state_census_data_center/census_2010/view.php

system.[81] It is already supported by law enforcement with the exception of the prison guards' union. The measure will come to the full legislature in a few months. Hopefully, some reforms will start putting justice back into the treatment of sex offenders. However, this is only a start and not a very popular issue politically. But reasonable minds may prevail. Much more needs to be done to not only curtail sexual abuse but also to redress former offenders' rights.

One thing is clear. Although released sex offenders have supposedly re-paid their debt to society by serving time, etc., new legislation enacted almost annually is making post-incarceration life more restrictive and much more dangerous for convicted *sex offenders*. In 1999, seven years **after** my conviction and two years **after** I completed probation, I was notified that information concerning my conviction would be made available to the public.[82] My photo and personal information, including my address, is posted on California's version of the Megan's List web site.[83] Anyone can access my information despite the fact that these federally

---

[81] http://www.leginfo.ca.gov/pub/11-12/bill/asm/ab_0601-0650/ab_625_
bill_20110527_amended_asm_v97.pdf

[82] http://en.wikipedia.org/wiki/Megan's_Law

[83] http://www.meganslaw.ca.gov/

mandated laws were non-existent when I was convicted (and played no role when I agreed to the "deal"). Article I, sections 9 and 10 of the Constitution of the United States are supposed to protect me from such **ex post facto** laws. I am still paying even more as a consequence of laws that were passed *six years* after my conviction.

That same year, I purchased an old home in my community that had been scheduled for demolition by the City. I sought and was granted a reprieve from demolition by the local Code Enforcement Authority so I could instead restore the property. I made immediate and substantial improvements. Following the renovation, I was recognized by the City Council and awarded our City's annual Community Improvement Award. I was heralded as a local hero in my community newspaper and neighborhood for turning the most run-down property into the crowning jewel of the street. Today, my wife and I live in that house.

In 2006, California voters passed Proposition 83[84] placing restrictions on *sex offenders* living within 2000 feet of a school or park. I live within 2000 feet of both a school and a park. The current State Attorney General's policy (supported by

---

[84] http://en.wikipedia.org/wiki/California_Proposition_83_(2006)

State Supreme Court rulings)[85] is I can remain in my home because of the *ex post facto* part of this law. But if I elect to move to a new location in California, I can't live within 2000 feet of a school or park. How is this not *double jeopardy* and complete disregard for due process? What if they decide to build a new school or park near where an offender lives? This is another example of injustice passed *fourteen years* **after** my conviction.

Although having a *convicted sex offender* in one's neighborhood probably isn't a comforting thought for anybody, one should consider the actual offense. The truth of the matter is there probably is not a single community in California that remains untouched by a **released** *sex offender*.

The Constitution protects individuals from being subjected to double jeopardy and ex post facto. However, elected officials are proving time and time again that the Constitution applies only to "**desirable**" individuals. Punishment for sexual assault should remain stiff and harsh, *offenders* should not be subject to vigilante justice. An individual should not have his personal liberties violated by having to confirm his residence annually

---

[85] http://ballotpedia.org/wiki/index.php/Jessica%27s_Law,_California_Proposition_83_(2006)

nor should he be branded with a "scarlet letter" by distributing his past criminal history to the public. Active police records are already kept in a database that is accessible to any law enforcement agency. That is where such information should be kept. For non-sex crimes, law enforcement agencies are not allowed to distribute personal information contained in their database to civilians. So why should they be encouraged to do just that for sex crimes? There is **no evidence** that disseminating this information freely has had any effect on protecting the public.[86]

We, as a society, depend on our Justice system to convict and assign punishment for crimes committed in our land. Once the individual has completed his punishment, he should be set free—totally free! Sure. A record should be kept of his conviction. But his rights and liberties should be completely reinstated. If the individual commits another offense, lock him up longer than before, perhaps even for life. But **until** the individual commits another crime, he should be set **free.**

It is time for the government to make use of CASOMB and other resources to evaluate the current system, clean up the registry and start using professionals to determine

---

[86] http://ipt-forensics.com/journal/volume11/j11_1_2.htm pg 15

the threats posed by individual offenders. It should not just create "blanket" laws to cover a whole class of people. To truly serve the public safety would be to properly assess each individual's risk periodically. Law enforcement resources would be utilized to better manage those few offenders that do pose a legitimate threat. In California, there are now tools to determine if an offender is HIGH RISK and/or a SEXUALLY VIOLENT PREDATOR.[87] Yet nothing is done to relieve the vast majority of low risk, non-violent offenders of being required to register—**especially for life!** In the "infinite wisdom" of the legislature, when it passed the original requirement, Superior Court Judges were empowered to require registration. But these same judges can't reverse or provide relief from their own rulings. Only the Governor can release anyone from this **lifetime** requirement. What Governor would take that kind of political risk? I could not find one instance in over 64 years where any governor released someone by pardon from the registry.

Sex offenders are lumped into one group. But the scope of sexual offenses is very wide and encompassing, from taking a

---

[87] SARATSO committee letters to the Governor http://www.cdcr.ca.gov/Parole/ SARATSO_Committee/SARATSO.html

photo of one's child playing in the bathtub to the most heinous crimes that receive widespread media attention. Because of the publicity given to the most horrific cases and the label, *sex offender,* attached to their perpetrators, all offenders on "the list" are stereotyped the same. Society's **worst**. Such labeling feeds the current, extremely hostile, political and societal attitudes toward **all** *sex offenders* without consideration of one's likelihood to re-offend. As a result a vigilante mindset creates a barrier to offenders who seek therapeutic help. Just the words *sex offender* evoke images of a sleazy person lurking around a schoolyard or un-kept vans cruising, looking for kids to grab. Those are very few. Thank God! But the term is used indiscriminately and unjustly covers many who have committed far lesser crimes.

I touched on this earlier, when I was talking about the murder analogy. Looking at it a different way, suppose a driver is intoxicated and causes a horrific accident resulting in multiple deaths. He is then described as a *traffic violator.* Similarly, a person who double-parks is also a *traffic violator.* We do not judge the double-parker in the same way we do the drunk driver. The term *traffic violator,* while valid, represents such a broad range of offenses that the term becomes meaningless.

Such is the case for *sex offenders*. The list encompasses such a broad range of offenders. How truly meaningful can it be? It amounts to nothing short of "black-listing" like the McCarthy era "Communist list."[88]

---

[88] http://en.wikipedia.org/wiki/McCarthyism

21

As I continue to re-integrate myself back into society, I have had many instances where my past has continued to cause me losses. I shared with you that I received the Community Improvement Award in 2000 for outstanding work on our home. How happy the neighborhood was that I had converted an eyesore into a 'jewel!' But a certain neighbor took it upon herself to go door-to-door and tell everyone else on the street about my conviction in spite of laws and disclaimers that are supposed to stop this kind of dissemination of information. They are spelled out right on the website. As a result, my wife and I are no longer invited to any of our block parties and are *shunned* in our own neighborhood. That particular woman and her husband divorced and each has moved on out of our neighborhood. But I am left with the "scarlet letter" and my wife suffering from no fault of her own.

I have chosen not to join any church. I have been offered and turned down membership in many Community Service

Clubs. I do not volunteer. I have even been suggested for local public office. Since I cannot pass a 'background' check I just politely decline all of them to the amazement of some.

I am FULLY RESPONSIBLE for my daughter's molest but I have **PAID MY DEBT.** I resent not being allowed to fully re-integrate back into society. I did not molest society. I have no desire to offend anyone. I remain available to my daughter/ victim to further resolve any issues she may want to pursue. But I owe society **NOTHING** beyond living as an upright, contributing member. PERIOD.

My counsel and I are currently pursuing a new course of legal action designed to have my conviction expunged (removed from the record). The strategy we are taking is (1) my original plea bargain is a binding *contract* between the State and myself.[89] In exchange for my pleading guilty and avoiding a costly trial, I was led to believe, under the law at that time, I would be able to have the case expunged after completing probation. The California Legislature changed the law in 1997 to make a Penal Code 288.5 conviction (mine) **unavailable** for expungement.[90] (2) For over fourteen years after entering

---

[89] http://cicchinilaw.com/PDFs/5-new-Ciicchini.pdf
[90] http://en.wikipedia.org/wiki/Expungement

into the contract the State has failed to fulfill its part of my "bargain" by changing the rules *after the fact* (ex post facto). If successful, my conviction would no longer be disclosed via a 'background check' which would make it dramatically easier for me to get business insurance, employment and bonding that, heretofore, have not been available to me. I would be allowed to access funding programs and take tax advantages for providing home health care for my wife. Currently, *registered sex offenders* are not considered suitable home health care providers (even though I'm married to the patient and no children are in the home). I am concerned about my ability to care for her needs as we get older and the possibility that her condition will deteriorate. But even if I prevail, I would **not** be released from registration. That is an entirely different matter. There was never a need for removal from the original list because it was never intended as a *punitive* measure but restricted only to being a *confidential* law tool.

This lifetime registration law is a sad commentary on the lack of judgment by our legislators. When faced with adopting federal mandates, instead of governing *for* the people and making modifications to the registry, they buckled and just went with the politically easy alternative with no regard to the unintended consequences. It's now time for them to step up and fix this miserable fucking mess. Then the public may realize some *actual* safety.

22

I persevered through challenging and difficult work to reveal and connect with my **true** self. I am eternally grateful to the doctor and all of my fellow group members that helped me work through "the valley of my life." I faced my worst fears and overcame my demons to be where I am today. After healing and change took hold in my life, I again contacted Alyssa. Together we explored my experiences and took small steps that led to our re-connecting. Over the course of many months we were able to move beyond "the past" and push forward into what has now become the most important relationship I have in this earthly life. We have been "back together" in excess of sixteen wonderful years. I count it a privilege and a blessing to have her by my side. I only hope I am able to be for her a fraction of what she is to me. She calls me her "diamond." I'd like to think it's because I'm valuable to her and not because I have a hard head!

All three of my children were impacted differently from the events that took place. I continue working to restore and nurture my relationship with each one as an adult. Sadly, the least developed is with Shelly and her two kids. For now, she has decided not to have any contact with me. She lives more than six hundred miles away. Alyssa and I have made several trips to her home and spent time talking about and *feeling* the past now that we are all adults. I believe she knows how remorseful I am for molesting her. She understands what the dynamic of our relationship was during her adolescent years. She continues to work to limit its influence in her life today.

I regret what I did. I am disappointed in myself and sorry that I did not give her the support, security and protection that a "healthy" father instinctively would have provided his children, especially his daughters. And so she doesn't fully trust me. I respect her for that. I have since never put her in an uncomfortable position, especially regarding her kids. My actions forfeited any real opportunity to have a deeper relationship with her or her children (my grandchildren). It is heartbreaking. But I respect all of my kids for shielding and protecting their children from any supposed threat. My hope is we all continue to move forward. I am committed and dedicated to that happening. However, there is a limit to how much responsibility I can demonstrate to Shelly. After many years, I have come to the place when I have "paid" a huge price for what happened and refuse to pay any more with regard to shame or emotional blackmail. I have left our relationship (or lack of one) up to her. Sometimes she wants one; sometimes she doesn't. She is in her mid-thirties and, just as in the case of her mother I stay "off the firing range." Her problems are beyond just my contribution. I sincerely wish her well in resolving them.

My son, Mark, is married to a lovely woman whom I take the opportunity to tease as often as I can just to see if I can stir up a reaction. But she is completely on to me after more than ten years. They have been blessed with three of their own sons. We are very proud of them. She is my favorite daughter-in-law. (Oops! She is my only daughter-in-law). Alyssa and I love her as our own.

Mark is a certified Microsoft Engineer, a civilian government employee enjoying a very successful career in IT (information technology) with the military. He and his family lack nothing and share lots of love. Alyssa and I are very happy for them. Often I am blessed to spend time with him as father and son. I love him. I remind him that his life differs from mine as he has a father who loves him and is not afraid to tell and show him frequently.

Ann amazes me. Being the youngest child she was impacted very differently than her siblings. She struggled in the shadow of all the chaos that took place during her childhood. She was only six when I gathered all three children together to tell them of the *first* divorce. That was her initial feeling of being abandoned. She wasn't even a teenager when the "bubble burst" about what I had done to her sister. From then on she lived (for legal reasons) without a Daddy actively participating in her life until she became an adult. Then her older sister moved out after taking care of her for several years. That was the second time she felt abandoned. Her brother left to live with me leaving her all alone to live with a mother that was unavailable to her needs. Abandoned yet again she married young. Her husband was also young. That proved to be too much to sustain a marriage. I am pleased to tell you she is now a single mother of a twelve year old daughter, educated through her own efforts and living independently. She has overcome much and we love her. She tackles anything dealt her way fiercely. I would want her on my side in any battle! She has pushed herself against big odds and succeeded. She makes me proud to call myself a father. She and her brother and sister **know** they are loved.

My greatest desire for my children and grandchildren is that each discovers the things that "shackle" him/her, that they learn to release the "chains of shame" destroying this miserable, multi-generational menace.

In many ways, my prayers are already answered. I awake each day renewed in the hope that we continue to move forward and grow rich in our relationships. If my life were cut short now, I can say that I was blessed by my wife, Alyssa, and my beautiful children and grandchildren. I am privileged to observe how my kids care for their own kids. I lack nothing. But like my bank account there is still room for more!

During the time I was being prosecuted, my brothers and sister were living all over the country. While I was in jail, they were not to be heard from and treated me as if I was no longer around. They had all the stereotypical attitudes that I continuously encounter when uninformed people are first confronted with a *sex offender*. Each one had to process for himself what I had done. They were reserved about asking questions and didn't want specific details. I have made myself available to answer anything and have had some meaningful conversations with them about my past. Our relationships continue to grow. We depend on each other now more than ever. We have all been blessed to still have our elderly mother to spend time with, too. We collectively count it a privilege to take care of her financial and material needs allowing her to live stress-free in her latter years. My plate is full running my businesses, providing for my employees, caring for my wife, mother, father-in-law and building my relationships with my family.

So to my sister and four brothers I say thank you for still loving me. We went through some tough times. And thank you for understanding why I wasn't at our father's funeral. Since my release from jail and my counseling, I have taken the lead in establishing a better relationship with each of them except my youngest brother. He is fifteen years younger than I and was raised by a step-mother after my parents divorced. I have a different and strange relationship with him. He keeps his distance from all of us and is struggling with his own life. He lives in another state. We rarely hear from him. Mostly he stays in contact with our mother. I wish him the best and, as time goes on, I hope we may re-establish a better relationship.

I like to remind all of my siblings that I love each of them. We hug when we greet each other and are able to express our feelings which differs significantly from our childhood. Recently, all six of us were able to be together and surprise our mother on her 85th birthday. It was the first time in over twenty years we were all with her at the same time. It was very touching and meaningful for our precious Mom.

Alyssa continues to struggle with her MS. Her enduring and persistent spirit shines most of the time. She restores my confidence, gives me hope and listens to my heartaches. She recharges my "battery" and encourages me. She is my biggest cheerleader. I only want to return to her love and gratefulness for all that she is because she is what completes me. My desire is to give her all I can to comfort and fulfill her life. Alyssa and I are fine and truly blessed. We have each other. She is my "beautiful queen." The world may label me a *registered sex offender,* but I'm **her** special registered citizen.

To summarize my journey, I was born and raised in a "normal" family. I learned subtle ways to get what I wanted by bending the rules. I made poor choices without much thought. I entered into a marriage without being mature enough or patient enough to evaluate my choice of a mate.

As my emotional needs weren't met, I gradually forced that part of my spouse's role onto my oldest daughter. I created a relationship largely to benefit myself at her tremendous expense. I was rightly prosecuted but wrongly charged. After paying 'society' I now live under the shadow of public scorn which causes me to always be on guard to protect myself and those I love from further harm via the dissemination of my *personal* information on the internet.

I am subjected to the ongoing changes in laws which hinder my ability to successfully re-integrate back into society and are in violation of ex *post facto* and other U.S. Constitutional provisions. I have paid a high price for my past behavior and caused much hurt and loss in my family. However, the costs keep rising as a result of the increasing reach of the "registry" being made available to the public.

The registered sex offender list was designed to be a tool used by law enforcement agencies, NOT the public. As it stands today, it is a confused mess that does nothing to keep children safe. Parents searching the Megan's Law websites have formed neighborhood vigilante groups and driven former offenders from their homes.[91] Those on the list are harassed by

---

91

cowardly neighbors who come in the night and use fear tactics to force them to leave. All such activity is ILLEGAL. Yet these so called do-gooders, in the name of protecting children, are harming the innocent children of the former offender. Trying to find a true predator on the registry is like trying to find a needle in a haystack without a magnet. Repeated studies have shown that most sex offenses (ninety-five percent) are NOT committed by a registered sex offender.[92] The majority of sex crimes are perpetrated by someone the victim knows.[93] This again proves the registry to be useless in helping the public protect their children. They have bought into the lies of the media and politicians who want to appear "tough on crime." Parents have failed to seek the facts available in many places like the US department of Justice and State agencies. *Sex offenders who have served their time, completed their parole or probation and received effective therapy should have another chance in society.*

This is not the first time in our history that we have singled out a segment of the population and punished it. In 1950, Senator Joseph McCarthy, in the midst of the nation's

---

[92] wikipedia.org/wiki/Sex_offender#Recidivism_rates
[93] CASOMB report on Homelessness (p10)

anti-communist hysteria, waved his infamous (and never identified) list of 205 "communists" working in the State Department.[94] He exploited the country's Cold War paranoia in pursuit of those he deemed "sympathizers."

We are once again "black-listing" the Americans known as sex offenders. We have allowed politicians to exploit our most vulnerable fear, the safety of our children, for political advantage. If we do nothing we are all responsible for allowing hysteria-driven legislation at the state and federal levels to continue unchecked. Voters must demand the truth from our elected officials regarding any legislation proposed to allegedly protect our children. Journalists have not asked hard-nosed questions or educated the public about the relative ease of how one becomes an offender, perpetuating the myth that all offenders are child molesters.

The majority of registered offenders have been convicted of "poor-behavior-choice" offenses which involved no victim. Most persons charged lack adequate funding to fight the charges. The resulting plea bargain is followed by automatic sex offender registration which permeates every aspect of one's life.

---

[94] http://www.heroism.org/class/1950/heroes/mccarthy.htm

Politicians seem to run amuck with this issue due to guaranteed press coverage and easy votes. Although a group of American citizens and their families are being blacklisted, banished and segregated, our politicians continue to pass more "scarlet letter" legislation. Banishment is **unconstitutional**.[95]

There is still a battle to be fought against ignorance, intolerance and indifference. If you are a citizen you have an obligation and a duty to question authority.

After more than twenty years following my plea conviction and my first-hand experience of being on the registry (with no foreseeable relief in sight), I think I'm able to shed some light on the effectiveness of this BS "list." Initially, notification laws were reactions to horrific crimes such as rape, murder or other violent assault. Contrary to public belief, the vast majority of sex crimes don't involve any of these. In fact, less than four percent of all sex offenses committed do.[96] There is a lack of data to even determine the *efficiency* of public notification. The system carries a big dollar cost and is ineffective at

---

[95] legal-dictionary.thefreedictionary.com/banishment
[96] CASOMB, report January 2010

lowering crime. It encourages vigilantism, compromises offenders' rights and subjects their family members to danger and it keeps growing exponentially. The public notification law is nothing more than legalized banishment and further punishment.

I have struggled to find and maintain housing and employment. I have personally overcome many of the roadblocks. But for the majority of *sex offenders,* it's another issue. There are many examples of professionals and others using laws beyond the way they were originally intended. For example, in some cases, law enforcement personnel have organized neighborhoods to exclude offenders from housing.[97] Inaccurate information has been released causing harm to offenders, their families and community members.[98] There are numerous documented cases of released *sex offenders* being thrown out of housing or losing jobs as a result of registration and notification laws.[99] Some have never been able to find jobs or housing. The increased risk of re-offending under stress due to the inability to settle into life in the community

---

[97] http://www.appa-net.org/eweb/docs/appa/pubs/RML.pdf
[98] Ibid
[99] http://www.hrw.org/news/2007/09/11/us-sex-offender-laws-may-do-more-harm-good

is a well-established phenomenon reported by those treating sexual abusers.[100] So how can one not consider the impact cruel, unusual and excessive punishment?

The best way to stop sexual abuse is to prevent it before it starts. Part of my motivation for sharing my story and experience with you is that you, the reader, may have found insight on my road and can look at your own a little differently, hopefully missing the pot-holes I hit head-on. I would like to think that the next time you hear the words *sex offender* you might take a step back and remember the Government has its' own *special meaning* for the terms—like making you a **Franchisee**!!

It's my prayer that if you are someone in an unfulfilling relationship, you will seek help or get out before you 'act-out' in anti-social behavior that may deteriorate into sexual abuse. *The consequences last a lifetime.*

The shame I referred to earlier has quieted down and no longer is a demon lurking in my soul. I prefer to call it 'healthy shame' that keeps me centered. I know who I am and, by now, you may know me a little better.

---

[100] http://criminaljustice.state.ny.us/nsor/som_mythsandfacts.htm

The cost to me for my offense long ago is the "cross" I bear. If any of what has happened in my life has been an eye-opener for you then my purpose for writing this book has come to pass. I cling and look forward to the slim chance that I may not reside on a public scorn list before I pass.

To some of you I hope this has been a challenge; to others I hope enlightening. To those special few, you might first have to remove the stick out of your balloon knot to "get it." (The rest of you can quit laughing now.) Thanks for hanging in there.

I welcome any comments or criticism that you
have and I can be contacted at:
R_Luther_Cooper@sbcglobal.net,
which of coarse is not my real name.

UPDATE: Since I completed this manuscript I've come across a recently released book entitled "*It's Okay We're Only Sex Offenders*" by Alan Rigby.[101] Alan is a committed "inmate client" at Coalinga State Hospital. He is designated as an SVP (sexual violent predator) under California Civil Commitment Law[102] which is the law used to extend a prisoners sentence. The States are now using this type of law to keep from releasing "sex prisoners" who were sane enough to stand trial but now after their sentences are completed are determined to have a *mental abnormality* that must be treated in a mental hospital—**indefinitely**!! Who's next—DUI's, traffic violators, politicians, parents, bad dressers, Franchisees? In Totalitarian States, they call them *political* prisoners. Throughout his book, he has peeled back the layers of deceit used by the Department of Mental Health in California in administering the SVP law. He says, "Nothing is as it seems."

---

[101] Alan Rigby, It's Okay We're Only Sex Offenders, Xlibris, 2008, Orders@ Xlibris.com

[102] dmh.ca.gov/services_and_programs/Forensic_Services/Sex_Offender_ Commitment_Program/FAQs.asp

"Sex offenders have been the scapegoat for a generation of ambitious politicians and a vindictive society. With the new advent of Civil Commitments, the nation has found a new way to justify imprisoning people for what they might do in the future. Where this will lead and what it has already accomplished is gradually coming to the surface.

Which group will become the next victims of community vengeance and psychological malfeasance? Has America taken over where Russia left off and violating its citizens' human rights? Are sex offenders truly these demonic pariahs and who are these SVPs (Sexually Violent Predators)? Are they the worst of the worst?" Alan Rigby.**103**

I strongly recommend reading this first-hand, factual account of California's Sexually Violent Predator Law and the men who have to endure the Civil Commitment *ruse*. Shame on the politicians and the Department of Mental Health that continue to use these new tactics to further their own agendas.

---

[103] It's Okay We're Only Sex Offenders, Alan Rigby, published 2008 Xlibris, back cover

Copies can be obtained by contacting Xlibris Corporation or overnight at on-line places like Amazon.com or Barnes and Nobel.

Xlibris Corporation 1-888-795-4274

www.Xlibris.com Orders@Xlibris.com

GET INVOLVED:

Reform of Sex Offender Laws.

Check out the following:

www.ReformSexOffenderLaws.Org   www.Californiarsol.org

www.voicesofthegulag.org   www.sosen.us/

www.//caorbl.org   www.satasort.org

SOLResearch.org   www.hibarso.com

http://oncefallen.com/index.html

http://sexoffenderresearch.blogspot.com/2007/09/laws-and-contacts-to—I have paid a high price for my past behavior and caused much hurt and loss in my family. However, the costs keep rising as a result of the increasing reach of the "registry" being made available to the public. assist-registrants.html

California recently (October 2011) established an advocacy group to push back against these blatantly discriminatory laws:

California Reform Sex Offender Laws (californiarsol.org)
MISSION STATEMENT:

The California Reform Sex Offender Laws organization is dedicated to restoring civil rights for those accused and/or convicted of sex crimes. In order to achieve that objective, CA RSOL will initiate and support legal action, legislation and public outreach.

Please consider going to their web page and supporting this effort by making a financial donation.

SOURCES

Board, California Sex Offender Management. "Adam Walsh Act."

Board, California Sex Offender Management. *HOMELESSNESS Amoung California's Registered Sex Offenders, An Update.* CASOMB, Augest 2011.

Board, California Sex Offender Management. "Recommendations Report January 2010."

Board, California Sex Offender Management. "Report on Gardner Case."

Christ, Youth For. "Youth For Christ Home Page Statement." 2011.

Danny. *Safe Net Response.* Northridge, CA: Safe Net Response, 2011.

Friedrichs, Ellen. *15 Shocking Tales of How Sex Laws Are Screwing the American People.* Alternet, June 2009.

Garcia, David Alire. "Prosecutors weigh reforms to state sex offender registry." *Michigan Messenger*, December 31, 2009.

Lieb, Scott Matson and Roxanne. *Sex Offender Registration: A Review of State Laws.* Washington State Institute for Public Policy, 1996.

Marshall Burns, Ph.D. *SOL Research, Research on sex offender laws and their effects on people and society.* SOLResearch.org.

Msg. I.S.Parrish, USA Retired. *Military Veterns PTSD Reference Manual.* Msg. I.S.Parrish, USA Retired.

Reimink, Troy. *Are Sex-Offender Laws in need of reform?* mlive.com, 2009.

Rogers, Laura L. *Sex Offender Regestry Laws: From Jacob Wetterling to Adam Walsh.* U.S. Department of Justice, July 2007.

"Sex Offender Supervision and GPS Monitoring Task Force."

System, Selctive Service. *History & Records, The Vietnam Lotteries.* Selective Service System, 2009.

Watch, Human Rights. *No East Answers.* Human Rights Watch, September 2011.

Board, California Sex Offender Management. "Recommendations Report January 2010."

Board, California Sex Offender Management. "Report on Gardner Case."

Lieb, Scott Matson and Roxanne. *Sex Offender Registration: A Review of State Laws.* Washington State Institute for Public Policy, 1996.

Marshall Burns, Ph.D. *SOL Research, Research on sex offender laws and their effects on people and society.* SOLResearch.org.

"Sex Offender Supervision and GPS Monitoring Task Force."

Kostas A. Katsavdakis, Marsha Weissman, and Alan Rosenthal. *Responding to Sexual Offenses: Research, Reason and Public Safety.* New York, NY : Center For Community Alternatives.

Other books I Recommended:

"How I Became a Registered Sex Offender" by Eric Smith

"We're All in This Together" by Frank Lindsay

"Once Fallen" by Derek Logue

CPSIA information can be obtained
at www.ICGtesting.com
Printed in the USA
LVHW031503170521
687659LV00002B/452